Printed in Hong Kong

ISBN 0 333 373065

First published in 1984 by
Macmillan Children's Books,
a division of Macmillan Publishers Limited,
4, Little Essex Street, London WC2R 3LF
and Basingstoke

Associated companies in
New York, Toronto, Dublin,
Melbourne, Johannesburg and Delhi

Designer
Julian Holland

Picture researcher
Stella Martin

Artists
Jim Marks
Sarah Pooley

Editors
Miranda Smith
Lynne Williams

Photocredits:
AGA Infrared Systems Ltd
All-Sport Photographic Ltd
Kaveh Bazargan
BBC
Biofotos
British Telecom
British Tourist Authority
Cable & Wireless PLC
Canon (UK) Ltd
Capital Radio
City of London Police
Bruce Coleman Ltd
Commodore
Concept Marketing & Communications Ltd
Electrosonic Ltd
Dr P Fenwick
Ferranti Electronics
Mike Fraser (Film Services) Ltd
Susan Griggs Agency
Hewlett Packard Ltd
Michael Holford
Alan Hutchison Library
Laserium at the London Planetarium
Stella Martin
Movalarm Television Surveillance Co Ltd
NASA
National Panasonic (UK) Ltd
Natural History Photographic Agency
Natural Science Photos
Picturepoint Ltd
Popperfoto
Post Office
Prestel
David Redfern
Rediffusion Simulation
Royal Greenwich Observatory
Science Photo Library
Sight and Sound
Smiths Industries
Nigel Snowdon
Spectrum Colour Library
Frank Spooner Pictures
Standard Telephones and Cables Ltd
Syndication International Ltd
Thomson EFCIS
Thorn EMI Ferguson
Trend Communications Ltd
John Watney
United Kingdom Atomic Energy Authority
ZEFA

The Science of
Communication
and Control

Lionel Bender

MACMILLAN

Contents

◁ The space shuttle in orbit above the Earth.

The brain

The brain is the body's centre of communication and control. It is responsible for both those actions which we can choose to do, such as running, talking and writing – and those that happen automatically, for example digesting a meal or the beating of the heart.

Information about our surroundings passes to the brain from the eyes, ears, nose, tongue and skin. The brain interprets these messages, makes decisions, and sends messages, via nerves, to the muscles to make the body run, throw a ball or move in some other way. The brain can also store information, so that we can remember things, and, most importantly, allows us to think, understand and form opinions.

▽ The brain is made up of two identical halves. For many actions of the body the brain acts as one, but for some there is a 'split' brain. For example, running (1) involves both sides; a skill such as painting (2) is controlled by the right side; and writing (3) and speech (4) are controlled by the left side of the brain. The hypothalamus, near the centre of the brain, deals with hunger (5), anger and fear (6).

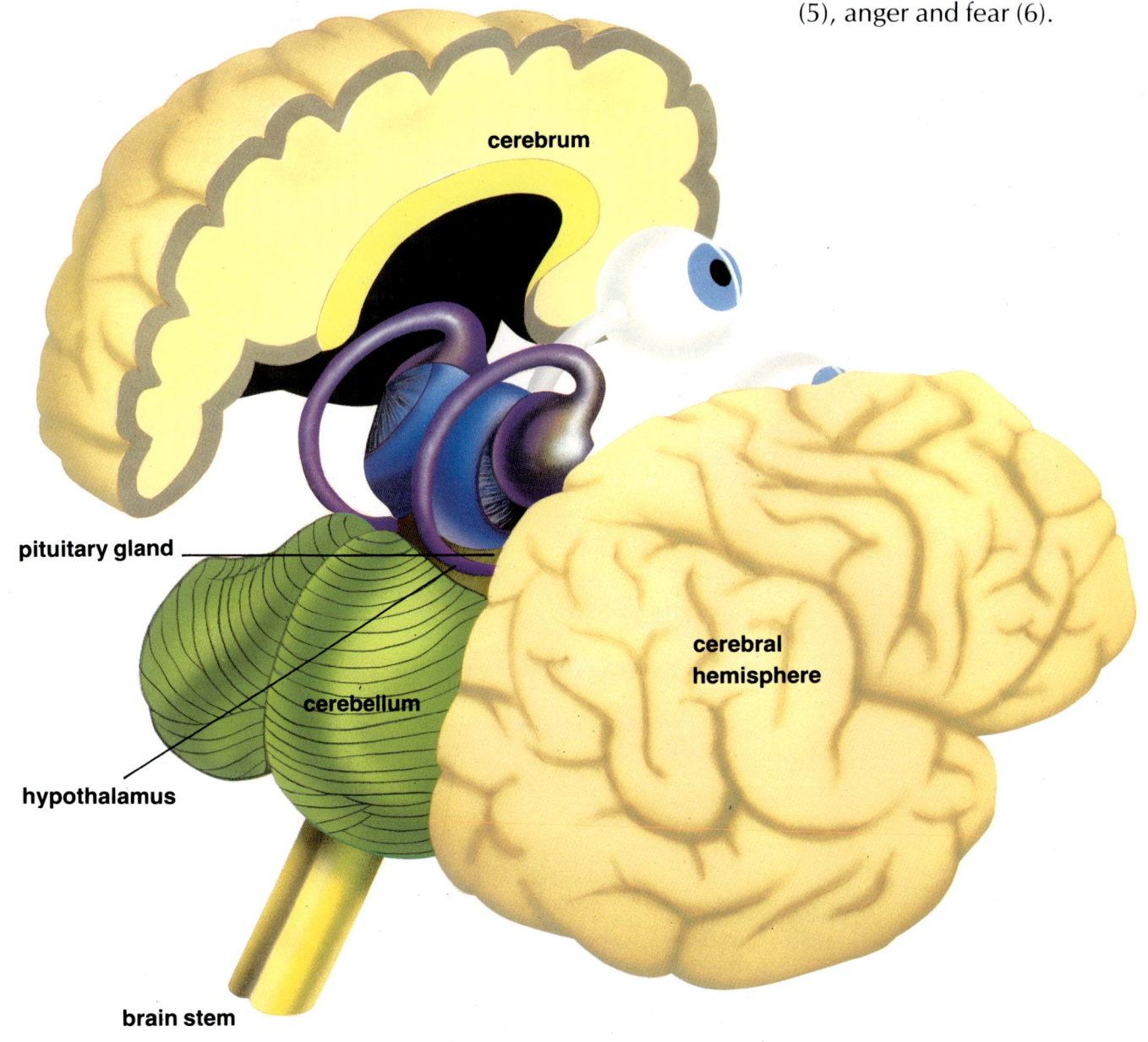

cerebrum

pituitary gland

cerebellum

cerebral hemisphere

hypothalamus

brain stem

▷ How is this Indian fakir able to lie on a bed of nails without feeling any pain? It is because 'mind' and 'body' communicate with and have control over each other in a complex manner. The brain is able to switch 'on' or 'off' messages coming to it from various parts of the body. Here, messages from pain and touch receptors in the skin have been ignored by the strength of the fakir's 'willpower'.

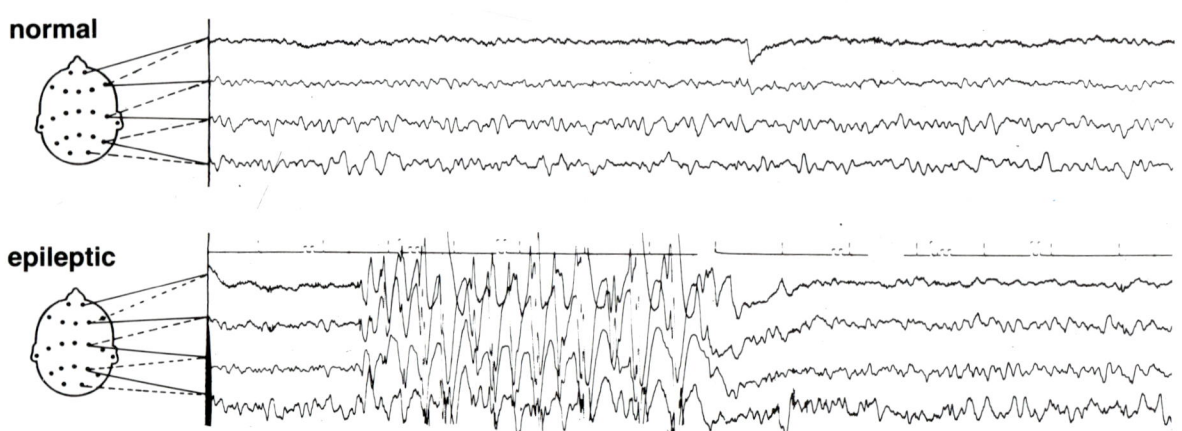

normal

epileptic

△ The brain is often compared to a computer or a telephone exchange because it can handle lots of messages at any one time. But the brain is similar to these electronic devices in another, more important way. The messages it receives and transmits are electrical too. Above are shown recordings of the electrical activity of the brain of a healthy ten-year-old girl and a girl with the brain disorder epilepsy.

Test your memory!

A picture of some everyday objects (*left*) and a telephone number (*right*).

Try to remember the objects and the number for a minute and then an hour.

The electronic era

Radios, televisions and washing machines all need electricity. They are all 'electronic' machines. In order to work, the electric current flowing through them must be controlled and channelled in special ways. Until about 1950, this was done using valves. A typical valve measures a few centimetres high and across. It has many parts and is difficult to make. Then transistors were developed. These work like valves but are made in a more simple way and each is tiny – only about the size of a match-head.

Silicon chips

The next step towards making the cheap, compact electronics of today was the development of the silicon chip. It is now possible to fit a complete electrical circuit – transistors, switches, resistors and capacitors – onto a tiny chip of silicon. A typical silicon chip measures only a few millimetres square. Inside the chip there are as many as 200,000 electrical parts.

△ These pocket calculators and other similar electronic educational toys contain one or more silicon chips. The calculators are, in fact, mini computers. Type in a simple mathematical problem, then try and solve it. The computer will check your answer.

◁ Many modern cameras are fitted with silicon chips. These focus the lens, adjust the size of the lens opening (the aperture) and alter the shutter speed automatically to control the amount of light entering the camera.

△ A diagram is being drawn of the electrical circuit to be placed on a silicon chip. The diagram is made hundreds of times smaller by a special camera until it is the same size as the chip. The photo produced is used to make a stencil. Using several different stencils, some of the chemical coating on the chip is etched away. This changes the flow of electricity through the chip.

▷ This instrument panel, fitted to new Austin Rover MG Maestros, contains silicon chips that produce spoken messages. It tells the driver when fuel levels are low or the engine temperature is too high.

As well as being very small, silicon chips work very fast and with very little power – a battery is enough. A typical silicon chip circuit operates in millionths of a second. This is faster than the speed at which the human brain works. In fact, some silicon chip instruments can work not only faster than the brain, but also more efficiently.

A powerful computer, for example, can receive thousands of facts and figures from several sources all at once. It can store the information, process it, then present it in any number of ways in only a second or two. However such machines can only do what they have been designed and instructed to do by people. Computer designers have not yet managed to build a machine which can think for itself.

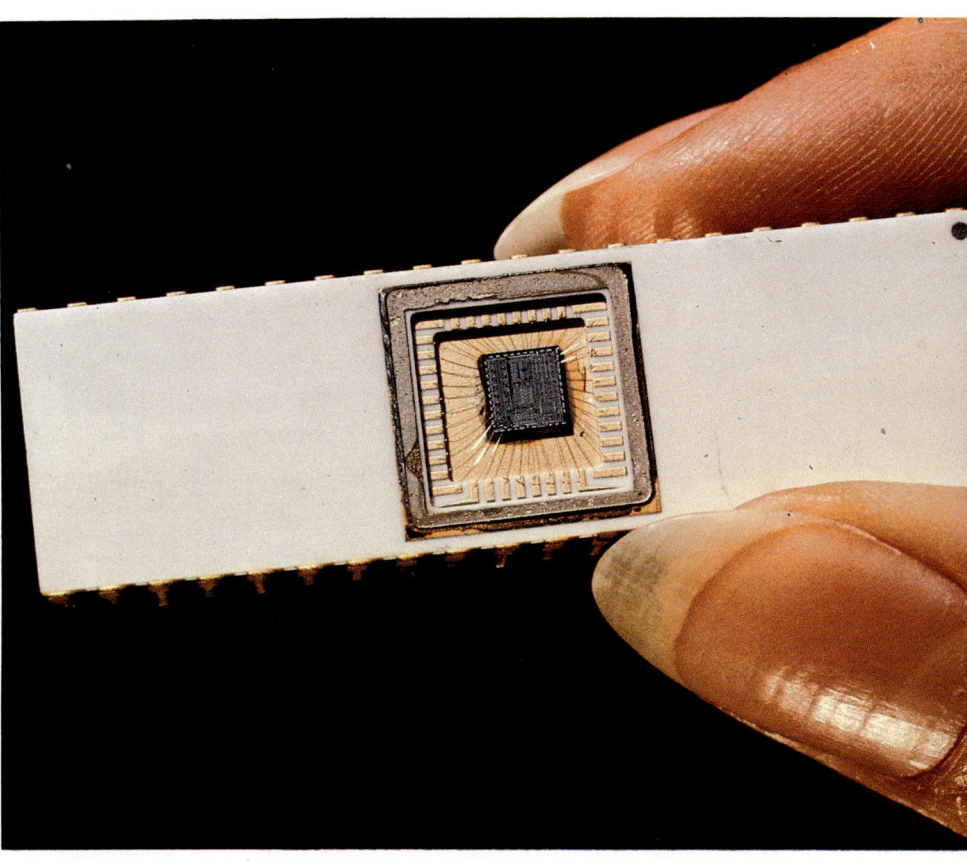

△ Under a microscope, thin gold wires are welded to tiny edge pads on a silicon chip. The wires will later be connected to the leads of the chip package *(above right)*.

△ A typical silicon chip package unit. Arranged in two parallel rows along the length of the package are small connector pins. These slot into holes in a printed circuit within the computer, washing machine or radio.

▷ This 'word processor' is an electric typewriter fitted with special silicon chips. The typist's rough draft is recorded in the machine's 'memory' chip. In another chip unit is a store of words, all spelt correctly. The word processor compares the typist's text with the built-in 'dictionary' and automatically types out the final, word-perfect text.

Computers

Computers are now commonplace in homes, schools, offices and factories. But from the £50 desk-top versions to the £1 million giants, they all work in the same simple way. A computer is nothing more than a silicon chip-instrument that can receive, store, process and transmit information. But its speed, the vast amounts of information it can handle and its faultless nature, make a computer far better than a human being for many jobs.

In the home, the main uses of a computer are for entertainment and education. Linked to a domestic television set and a portable tape recorder, a home or 'micro' computer can be used to play *Space Invaders* or *Alien Attack*. You can even play chess or draughts with one, with the computer as your opponent.

Slightly larger, more powerful computers – minicomputers – are used in offices. They are needed for financial planning and production of invoices and receipts, and in schools for timetabling and keeping records and exam results of pupils. In factories for example, in a car assembly plant, a central computer may receive information from and control a series of mini-computers.

△ A typical 'electronic' office. A word processor, a special word-handling computer, is being used to compose and print out hundreds of copies of a standard letter, automatically changing the name and address on each copy. The client's details and the secretary's instructions are all stored in the computer's memory.

◁ A computer's speed and accuracy in handling lots of information makes it useful in aircraft flight. In this cockpit of a test aircraft, the TV/calculator-like unit on the left is a computer system capable of doing the same job as all the instruments on the right of the cockpit.

◁ To get started with home computing, all you need is a computer unit and a television set. The computer usually includes a typewriter-like keyboard and the information-handling and memory units.

You work the computer by typing in instructions using the appropriate programming language. You can buy pre-recorded programs on tape, feeding these into the computer using a cassette recorder. Most home computers can produce exciting colour graphics and a range of sounds.

A computer can handle both words and figures. For example, you can type into a computer hundreds of different names and addresses and then instruct the machine to provide you with an alphabetical list. Or you can feed in all of a Saturday's soccer results and get the computer to produce the up-to-date league tables. But whatever you instruct the computer to do, it will operate only by subtracting, adding or comparing the pieces of information it holds in its memory. This is because computers work on an either/or, on/off or yes/no system.

Computer languages

Computers use a binary (two parts) code. Each letter, symbol or number on the computer keyboard is represented inside the computer as a pattern, or code, of 0s and 1s. 0 is off, 1 is on. To communicate with a computer using the binary code is rather difficult. We are not used to talking and writing in numbers! So special languages have been developed to allow us to translate ordinary English into the computer's working language. To instruct a computer to perform a task you must first write a set of instructions or program using one of these languages.

▽ Most home computers use the programming language BASIC. Notice how the instructions are numbered in sequence. The computer's logical system follows the sequence exactly.

```
10    REM ***DIARY***
20    REM BY SUSAN CURRAN
30    CLS
40    REM SET UP DATA ARRAYS
50    DIM D1$(6): DIM O1$(6)
60    FOR X = 1 TO 6
70    READ D1$(X): READ O1$(X)
80    NEXT X
90    DIM D2$(6): DIM O2$(6)
100   FOR X = 1 TO 6
110   READ D2$(X): READ O2$(X)
120   NEXT X
130   DIM D3$(6): DIM O3$(6)
140   FOR X = 1 TO 6
150   READ D3$(X): READ O3$(X)
160   NEXT X
170   REM OBTAIN DATE TO CHECK
```

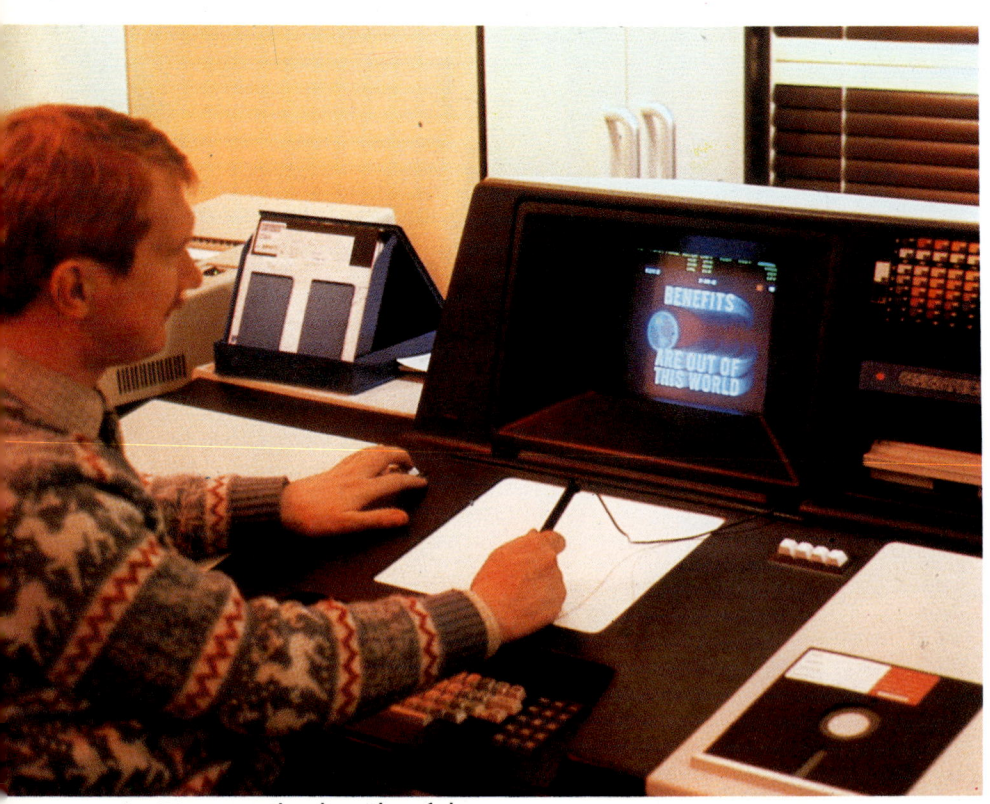

△ Given only details of the overall shape and size of, say, a car, building or even the human body, a computer can produce a three-dimensional view of that object.

In this picture a 'graphics' computer is being used.

△ Once an image is stored in the graphics computer's memory, the operator can paint it in any combination of several thousand colours. He can also make the image move, as with this computer picture of a dancer.

Count up to 1,000 on your fingers!

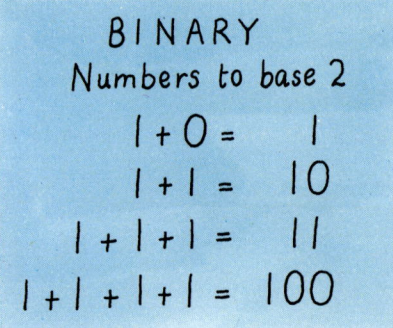

BINARY
Numbers to base 2

$1 + 0 = 1$
$1 + 1 = 10$
$1 + 1 + 1 = 11$
$1 + 1 + 1 + 1 = 100$

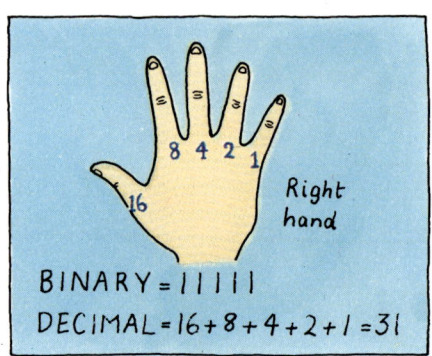

Right hand

BINARY = 11111
DECIMAL = 16 + 8 + 4 + 2 + 1 = 31

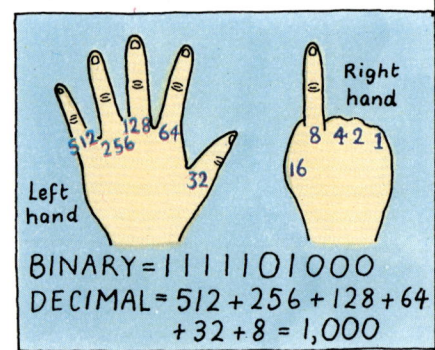

Right hand

Left hand

BINARY = 111110 1000
DECIMAL = 512 + 256 + 128 + 64 + 32 + 8 = 1,000

Computers do their sums in binary, using 0s and 1s. Using

binary, count up to 1,000 on your fingers. Going from left

to right each finger is worth double the previous one.

12

Time and change

All things change with time. Some, such as the size of a tree, change slowly. Others, for example the position on the road of a moving car, change quickly. In fact, we are aware of the passing of time simply because we can see such changes or processes happening. In communication, the passage of time is important as we need to know *when* someone said or wrote something. It may also be important to control *when* something changes.

Time scales

There are many different time scales. The internal structure of atoms, the invisible building bricks of all matter, changes with every millionth of a second. A bacterial cell grows and divides in two every few minutes. The position of the Sun in the sky changes with each hour. Geology, the study of the Earth's structure, has a time scale involving tens of thousands of years. Astronomy deals in millions of years.

◁ 9 o'clock on London Bridge on a typical weekday morning. Commuters, having left home at between 7.45 and 8am as usual, arrive by train at London Bridge Station and rush into the City for work.

At 9.30 precisely the doors of the banks open for another day's business. By 10am, in shops and offices everywhere all are hard at work. At 11am it is time to break for a cup of tea and a chat. Perhaps a meeting at 12 or 12:30pm breaks up the morning routine. Then back to work until 1pm. An hour for lunch.

An eye is kept on the watch or clock so as not to be late for the afternoon return. Back to the office by 2pm. The second tea-break of the day is at around 4pm. At 5pm a flood of people will be moving across London Bridge in the opposite direction, everyone running to catch the train home. Monday to Friday, 52 weeks of the year, the story is the same. Just like clockwork. Our lives seem ruled by time.

◁ Big Ben, London. The clock mechanism of huge wheels and springs is not wound with a huge key but by an electric motor. Within such a 'mechanical' clock mechanism there are three main elements. A mainspring, using a system of toothed wheels and cogs, produces a turning force. Another system of wheels controls its speed.

Lastly, a system of gears transmits the motion of the mainspring to the hands of the clock.

△ This fossilized tree section is two clocks in one. The first clock tells us the tree's age when it died; each ring represents one year's growth. The second clock tells us how many thousands of years ago the tree lived.

The chemical element carbon 14 in the tree decays slowly with time into ordinary carbon 12. By measuring and comparing the amounts of these two types of carbon, scientists can tell the fossil's age.

There are many different ways of measuring time. However, each involves the comparison with an event that occurs regularly and at fixed intervals.

For example, a pendulum clock uses as a standard the time taken for the pendulum to swing back and forth. A sundial measures time in relation to the apparent movement of the Sun in the sky. A sandglass or 'egg-timer' is designed so that it takes a fixed period of time for all the sand to fall from one half into the other. A digital watch measures time on the basis of the vibrations of a tiny piece of quartz crystal.

The accuracy of all these clocks varies a lot – a sundial is accurate to within only a few minutes, a digital watch to within $\frac{1}{50}$ second.

▷ An atomic clock based at the Royal Observatory, Greenwich. Atomic clocks work by counting the natural, very regular to-and-fro movements of particles within certain atoms. They have an accuracy of within one ten thousand millionth of a second per day.

Make a sundial!

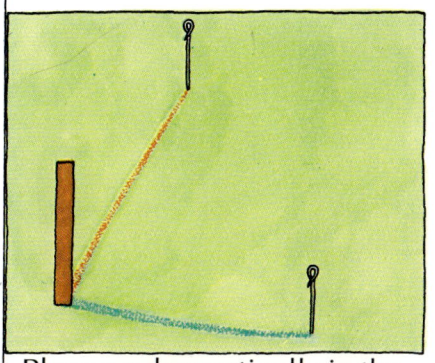

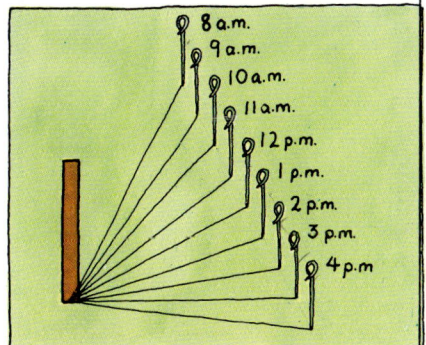

Place a ruler vertically in the ground. At 8am, put a peg at the top of the shadow of the ruler. Repeat at 4pm. Mark out eight equal divisions between the first two pegs. Stretch cotton from the ruler to each peg to mark out the hours.

Chemical messengers

Chemicals can act as both communicators and controllers. In most animals fast, short-term changes or actions are brought about by the nervous system. But slow, long-term changes such as growth are the work of special natural chemicals known as hormones.

Each hormone is secreted from a cell or tissue in one part of the creature and brings about changes in another, distant part. For example, the hormone insulin is secreted by the pancreas gland into the bloodstream. It flows round the body. When there is too much glucose in the blood, it stimulates the liver and muscles (but no other organs) to remove glucose from the bloodstream. Another hormone, glucagon, has the exact opposite effect.

Insulin and glucagon together control blood sugar levels. If either or both of these are lacking, as is insulin in the case of diabetics, the patient may suffer from weakness and loss of weight.

Plants and animals

Plants, too, produce hormones. Some control the time and rate of growth of roots, stems, leaves and flowers. Others make sure that leaves grow towards the light and roots towards water.

Certain animals use other natural chemicals just for communication. A dog will often urinate on a lamp-post or tree within its territory. Other dogs, on smelling the urine, will know not to stay too long in the area.

▷ In the life cycle of butterflies and moths, special chemicals control the change from caterpillar to pupa to adult. Released by a gland near the caterpillar's head, the chemicals spread to all parts of its body. They bring about a major rebuilding of the caterpillar's body. A crawling 'feeding machine' becomes a delicate flying creature.

◁ As with dogs, male impala use urine as a chemical messenger to mark their territory. Here a male has just urinated on a bush.

◁ A policeman is using a breathalyser to test if the car driver has been drinking too much alcohol and is unfit to drive. Most breathalysers use 'indicators', chemicals which change colour with different conditions. If the driver's breath is free of alcohol, the indicator remains colourless. If the alcohol level is too high, the indicator changes colour, usually to a shade of green.

Chemical messengers are to be found not only in the sciences of biology and chemistry. In medicine, for instance, chemicals that are only mildly radioactive are used as 'tracers' to find diseased organs and tissues in the body which are not working properly. Scratches on the cornea of the eye are detected using fluorescein which, dropped in the eye, stains the surface just where it is damaged.

Photography

Perhaps the most important of all chemical messengers are those used in photography. Photographic papers and films are coated with tiny grains of chemicals known as silver halides. When exposed to light, the grains form minute dark specks of metallic silver. Developed and fixed, the film shows light and dark areas corresponding with those of the original image.

▷ The man in the centre stands 2.82 metres tall. The man on the right is only 0.9 metres tall. Their companion is of average height, 1.75 metres. The difference in their size is due mainly to the effect of growth hormone. This is a chemical produced by the pituitary gland in the brain.

The hormone flows to all parts of the body. If the body produces too much growth hormone during childhood, the person becomes very tall. Too little of the hormone and normal height is never reached.

Animal language

Among social animals, of which the best-known are ants, bees and mammals such as dolphins, monkeys and Man, individuals must have a way of communicating with one another. They need to tell each other where to set up their territory and how it should be defended against other groups and against enemies. They need to let each know about suitable places to build a home or to find food so that they do not become overcrowded or use up a good food source too quickly.

Any system used by a social group to communicate in some way is called a language. There are many different kinds of language. By far the most flexible and expressive animal language, though, is human speech. Other animals use a language involving sounds, but none of them has such a vast 'vocabulary'. For example, the English vocabulary runs into thousands of words. Man's closest relatives, the gorillas, chimpanzees and orang-utans, have a 'spoken' language with no more than twenty different sounds.

▽ Clearly only two of these people are communicating. How are they doing this? Simply by speaking to one another. Human speech is unique in the animal world. It involves not only a wide range of different sounds but also the ability to combine language with complicated ideas and thought.

△ This knife-fish generates tiny pulses of electricity to find its way around and to communicate. The pulses set currents flowing in the surrounding water. Objects in the water – rocks or another fish – reflect the currents. The knife-fish works out from them what objects it is near.

▷ Bottlenose dolphins, known to Americans as porpoises, are star performers. Not only are they agile swimmers, they also use a language similar to our own. The dolphins' attendants train them using whistles and singing notes similar to the animals' calls. Dolphins can 'talk' to one another over tens of kilometres.

△ These worker honeybees communicate with one another using dance language. A foraging bee, having found some flowers with nectar, returns to the hive. A round dance on the surface of the honeycomb tells the other bees that the flowers are less than about 80 metres from the hive and so are easily found. A waggle dance tells them not only that the flowers are some distance away – the slower the dance the further away they are – but also their direction from the hive.

△ A prairie dog makes an alarm call. Prairie dogs are hamster-like, short-tailed squirrels that live on the plains of North America. They live in groups of up to ten individuals.

Prairie dogs use a variety of calls to communicate with one another and to defend their territory. To advertize its group's territory, a prairie dog will rear up on its hind legs and, with nose pointing to the sky, produce a series of two-syllable calls.

A different type of call is used by the prairie dog as an alarm signal. When it sees an enemy – mainly coyotes, eagles and hawks – a prairie dog will utter a short, high-pitched sound that sends all its companions bolting for cover. At times, this call sounds like a bark, which is why the animals are called prairie dogs.

Talking without words

We communicate with each other in many ways other than by speaking. We use lots of gestures, postures, facial expressions and displays to let others know about things such as our mood or feelings. Young children, even before they are able to talk, communicate with their parents with smiles, frowns, grimaces, gasps, groans of pain and cries of delight.

Almost all of these messages are visual. Many other animals also use visual languages. Chimpanzees, for example, produce facial expressions much like our own. A smile expresses happiness, although it can be 'put on' and conceal fear or dislike. A stare, with mouth firmly closed, communicates anger or aggression. In order to threaten another individual, a snake may vibrate the end of its tail, or a European toad will inflate its lungs to appear bigger than it really is. To court a female, a male jumping spider will wave its fore limbs in a special pattern and a male peacock will spread out its colourful tail feathers.

Body language

Examples of 'talking without words' are not always so obvious. For instance, are you aware of the body language we use when we meet one another? If someone greets another with head bent low, shoulders forwards, arms by the sides and is taking small shuffling steps, he or she is clearly rather shy or perhaps depressed or sad. If, on the other hand, the person holds his body and head up, swings his arms and remains balanced and in control, he or she is confident or happy.

△ A footballer, having scored a goal, turns to his team-mates in triumph. With arms raised — a victory display — and shouting in excitement, his actions contrast with those of the opposition. They are probably walking back to their positions with heads low and arms down by their sides — sure signs of defeat.

◁ This child's upturned, slightly open mouth — a smile — shows that she is happy. Such facial expressions can often communicate a person's feelings much quicker than words.

Unlike spoken languages, the vocabulary of our gestures and facial expressions are almost truly international. A smile or a frown is recognizable to everyone. However, there are some gestures that have different meanings in different countries. A compliment to one person may be an insult or even nonsense to another. For example, the 'thumbs-up' sign, meaning excellent, will be understood by an American but not by, say, a Malaysian.

◁ Tears flowing from his eyes, his mouth open and down-turned and with wrinkled forehead. Clearly this little boy is very sad. Anger, fear, surprise and disgust are other feelings that we show by the expression on our face.

▷ A lioness puts on a threatening display as an enemy approaches. Her fierce look, with mouth open to show her menacing teeth, is usually enough to frighten off the attacker. She has probably just made a kill to provide food for herself and her cubs.

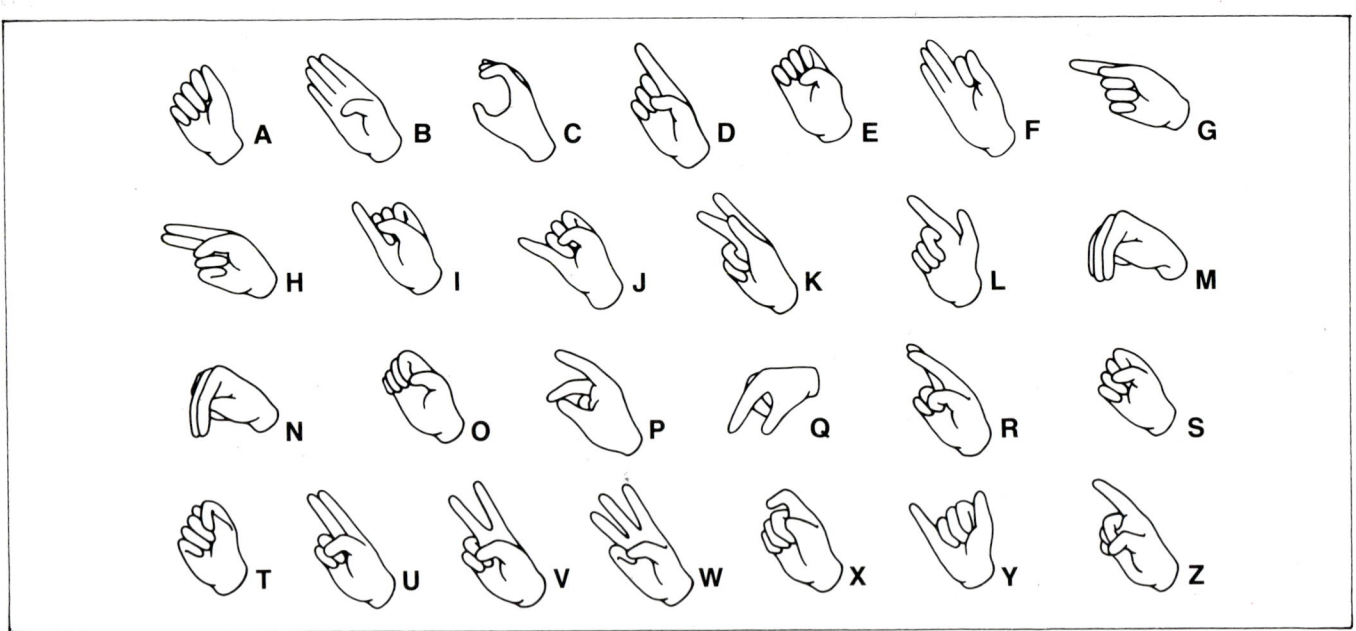

△ People who cannot hear or speak can communicate with one another using their fingers and hands to illustrate the letters of the alphabet. This chart illustrates the deaf and dumb language.

◁ A male Manchurian crane woos a female crane with a very elaborate courtship display.

Many animals, but particularly birds and mammals that live in social groups, often communicate with one another using body movements. The male bird, seeking a mate, walks round the female with quick stiff-legged steps and wings half-spread. The female 'replies' by spreading her wings.

Signs and signals

When we speak to someone, we use a vast range of different sounds. Facial expressions depend on tiny changes of the shape of the mouth, eyes, nose and cheeks. Gestures involve a pattern of movements of the arms and hands. But there is a particular type of communication where one, still image conveys the message.

Road signs, for example, are easily recognizable and understandable. A round sign always spells out an order – 'No entry' or '50 mph maximum speed'. A rectangular-shaped sign provides information such as the direction of roads leading from a roundabout. A triangular-shaped sign carries a warning to drivers.

Of course, some of these signs use words as well as graphics. Other examples of instant visual communication use only graphics – a football team's colour strip or railway signals. In the insect world, some butterflies have false 'eyes' which stop birds from eating them. Some flies have markings like those of a wasp and so give the impression of being harmful.

△ A gendarme in Paris controls the traffic at a busy junction. He uses hand signals to tell drivers whether they should stop where they are or if they can proceed. Holding his arm out to one side signals 'stop' to traffic from behind, and 'go' to traffic wanting to turn right.

◁ A warning sign to car drivers. Beware! The road ahead runs alongside a river or canal. The message is understood immediately.

◁ Punks in King's Road, Chelsea, London. With their hair dyed, cut and styled in strange ways, their ear and nose-rings and pins, and their torn and tattered clothing, they communicate their status in a striking manner.

They have developed a uniform, much in the same way as City businessmen have made the pin-striped suit and umbrella the standard way of dressing for work in a bank or Civil Service office.

▷ Flags of countries and symbols of large international organizations are used to convey a message of common interest among people. These men and women are carrying posters with the symbol of the CND, the Campaign for Nuclear Disarmament. Their message is 'Ban the bomb'.

Other equally famous symbols include those of the Red Cross Organization and the World Wildlife Fund. Do you know them both?

▷ This Malaysian hawkmoth caterpillar has eyespots which it uses as a signal to frighten off its enemies. When the caterpillar is disturbed it draws in the front of its body and makes the false 'eyes' stand out. It then looks like the head of a venomous snake!

▽ Semaphore is a system of signalling using two flags, or lights, to send messages. The flags are held with straight arms and the angle between the flags denotes the letter. Semaphore is mainly used by ships at sea.

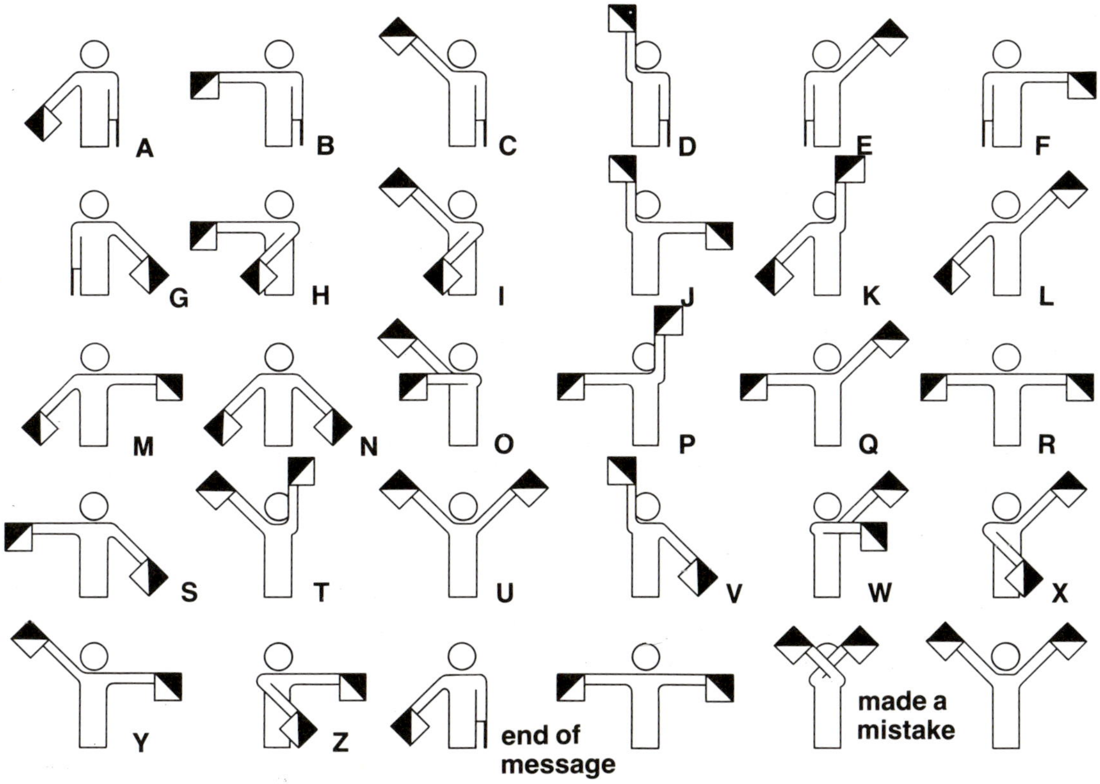

A   B   C   D   E   F

G   H   I   J   K   L

M   N   O   P   Q   R

S   T   U   V   W   X

Y   Z   end of message   made a mistake

Codes and secret messages

Speech and writing are 'open' forms of communication. A conversation can be overheard and a book can be read by any number of people. Similarly, road signs and animal warning displays are for all to see. Getting the message across using, say, a system of holes punched in a paper tape is more secret.

Secret messages

There are several ways of hiding a message. A letter can be written using invisible ink. You can try this yourself using lemon juice. Dip an old pen or a thin stick into some juice from a fresh lemon and write your message on a clean piece of ordinary white paper. Let the juice dry; the paper will be transparent where you wrote on it. Then ask an adult to warm the paper carefully over a hot radiator or a small flame on a cooker. Your message will show up as a brown colour.

The letters and words of the message could also be changed in some way. For example, individual letters can be mixed up so that the message can be read only when they are unscrambled in a set fashion. Such messages are known as cyphers. Or the letters can be changed into numbers or symbols to form a code. Messages written in code form are to be found in a whole variety of everyday situations.

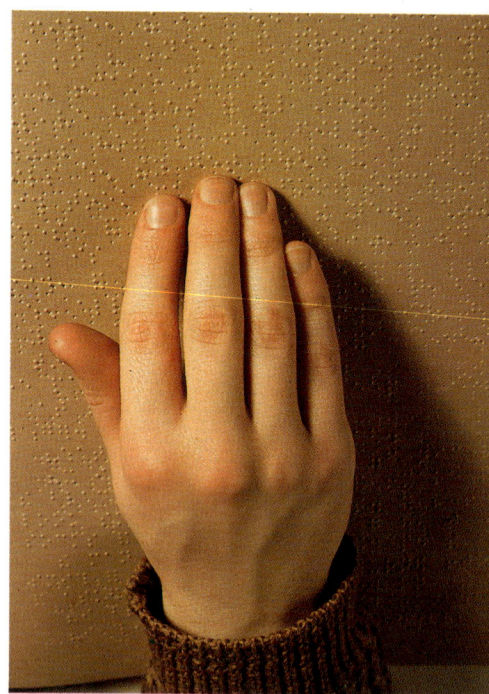

△ People who cannot see can read using braille. Braille is a code made of a different pattern of raised dots for each letter of the alphabet. The right hand is used to interpret the code, while the left hand feels for the beginning of the next line.

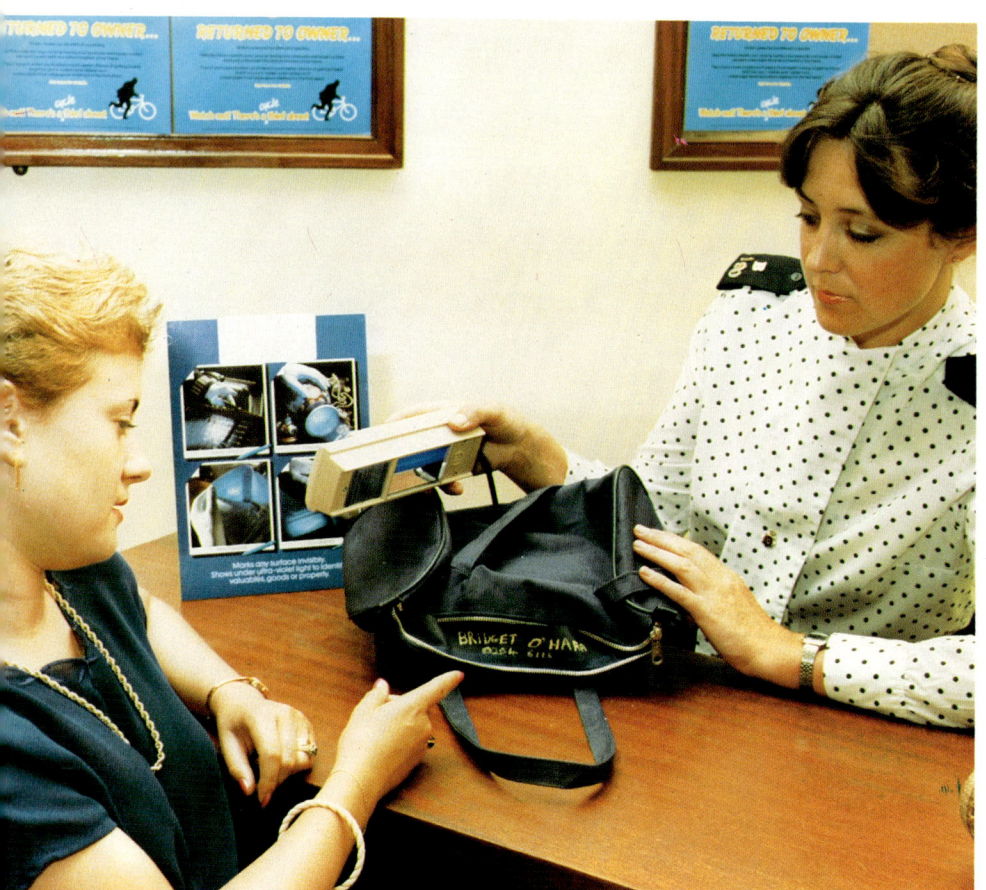

◁ A policewoman holds an ultraviolet lamp over a handbag, revealing the owner's name and telephone number written with invisible ink. This does not show up under ordinary light but when lit with ultraviolet light it becomes visible.

28

How organs work

△ ◁ An old-fashioned organ plays music by converting a code of holes punched in cards into musical notes. As the organ wheel turns, the cards are pressed against a cylinder covered with tiny pins.

The pins can move up and down. Where there are holes in a card, the pins push through them. As they do so, they push down on keys that produce the notes.

◁ This mushroom-like structure is a radio navigation beacon. It stands on the deck of a cable-laying ship. Its job is to help work out the ship's position by interpreting coded information received from a navigational satellite. In one of these navigation systems eight satellites orbit the Earth continuously, passing over the North and South poles with each circuit.

A card-trick!

Each of ten players picks up and looks at a pair of cards, then replaces them.

As trickster, pick up the cards in pairs. Then set them, face up, as in the code.

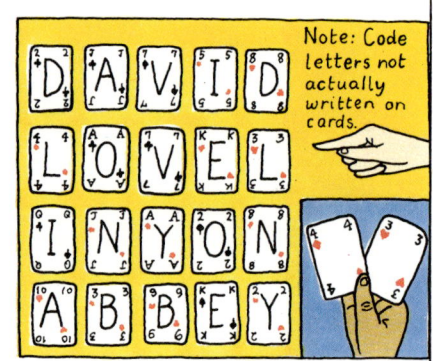

Ask each player the row or rows of their cards. Matching code letters reveals their pairs.

Copying and reproducing

Control means to rule or have power or to influence someone or something. To be able to copy something means having a high degree of control. For instance, to mass produce cars all to a particular design from a random collection of nuts, bolts and sheets and blocks of metal, one must make sure that all the parts are of a standard shape and size and are brought to the production line in the correct order and at the correct time. This area of car manufacture is known as production control.

To turn out thousands of blocks of cheese all looking, smelling and tasting just as they should involves another type of control. A careful check must be made that the ingredients are all fresh and are used in the correct amounts. So this is what is meant by quality control.

Control is also involved in the reproduction of animals and plants. When, for example, cars are copied, all 'offspring' are

▽ A sea of cars? No, just the 'warehouse' at one of British Leyland's car manufacturing plants. Modern car assembly is fast and accurate. Each week, thousands of cars (all identical to one another) roll off the production line. Thousands of workers are involved.

identical to one another, but in reproduction usually they are not. A cow always gives birth to a calf and never a lamb. But the calf is never an exact copy of its mother.

DNA

Reproduction is clearly a complicated process. A 'blueprint' contained within all living cells makes sure that it all goes according to plan. This takes the form of a code, the genetic code, within a special biological building brick known as DNA or deoxyribonucleic acid.

The code exists as a sequence of chemicals within the DNA. The sequence can be 'copied' and passed from one cell to the next during normal cell division. In animal and plant reproduction, though, where two 'sex' cells, the male and female, must join to form the new indivdual, the code is passed on after it is changed very slightly. This accounts for the differences between the cow and its calf or, equally, your parents and yourself.

▷ A microscopic view of a colony of bacteria. Bacteria are one of the simplest forms of life. They are present everywhere in vast numbers on the Earth's surface. Each bacterium consists of only a single cell. Given ideal conditions, a bacterial cell can grow very fast, dividing once every half an hour.

Within a day one bacterium can produce tens of millions of new cells. An example of how fast bacteria can grow is the way that milk can seem fresh one day and the next is a murky, smelly undrinkable goo.

◁ Orange drink is being bottled for sale in supermarkets. This is 'copying' on a large scale. It involves control both of the manufacturing processes and of supply of oranges to the factory and bottles to the shops.

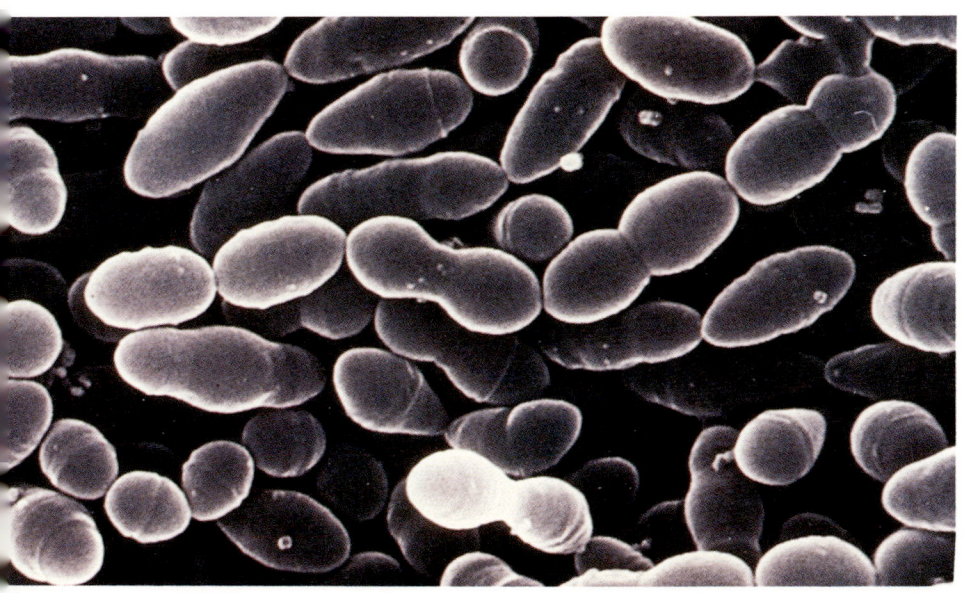

▽ *Throw a ball into the clown's mouth to win a prize!* It does not matter with which clown this girl tries her luck because they are all the same. They are just copies made from a standard mould. A mould is a hollow vessel of a particular shape – in this case, a clown's head and shoulders – into which a melted substance, such as metal or plastic, is poured. When the substance cools it takes the mould's shape. Many objects are made from moulds.

Books, magazines and newspapers

Despite the invention of television and radio, the printed word is probably still the best way of communicating. Everyday, millions of newspapers are bought and read. They tell us what is happening (or has just happened) around the world. The 'news' on television or radio rarely lasts more than half an hour. As it tries to mix national and international news, it can only cover a tiny amount of the day's events. A newspaper has no such restrictions.

Books

Books communicate in many different ways. A novel provides entertainment on a long train journey or for a cold winter's night best spent at home. Encyclopaedias are great stores of useful facts and figures. They can be referred to instantly time and time again to find the answers to questions related to work or school studies or to settle disputes that arise when playing quizzes with family and friends.

▽ Picture comics are a means of communication too. Here a comic is a source of interest and entertainment for a group of children in São Paulo, Brazil. Perhaps only one of them can read the words but, with the help of the picture strips, the story can be revealed to all.

▷ A newsagent in London displays his newspapers and magazines to catch the eye of passers-by. Not only does he sell *The Times*, *Telegraph* and *Guardian* but also foreign newspapers such as *Le Figaro* from France, the German newspaper *Die Weldt* and the *New York Times* and *Los Angeles Times*. When people travel abroad they often need to keep in touch with what is happening at home. Buying their usual daily paper is the best means of doing this.

▷ Within 100 metres of this bookshop in Charing Cross Road, London, there are perhaps 50 other bookshops, several public libraries and a number of specialist book collections housed in museums.

Computers may indeed one day replace books, but books are still the best means of storing and communicating large quantities of information for a large number of people. A weighty tome can store a million words and perhaps 500 pictures.

For those of us who cannot find the time to read a newspaper or a book, magazines are the answer for the printed word. Most Sunday newspapers, and now some 'daily's', come with their own magazine. Filled with colour photographs and both serious news articles and entertaining 'features', to say nothing of cookery recipes, cartoons and a wealth of adverts, they are usually kept for interest or reference when the newspaper has long been thrown away. Many of them provide several days' reading.

Specialist magazines – computing, photography, model railways, knitting, travel and so on – provide those keen on hobbies with details of the latest products, ideas for projects and useful addresses.

The importance of print

But the influence and importance of the printed word goes beyond the world of newspapers, books and magazines. In advertizing, printed posters and brochures are used to communicate the features of a new product. A small company, to make itself known to the general public, will distribute printed business cards or leaflets to every home in its area. A museum produces wallcharts and information packs as educational aids. Worksheets, syllabuses, timetables and exam papers are part and parcel of school life.

In offices, schedules and memos are everyday reminders of the power of the printed word, as are gas, electricity and telephone bills.

◁ Newspaper reporters and photographers – along with television and radio recording crews – crowd around President Mitterand of France at a press conference.

Each morning, reporters are sent out to collect information about the day's events. Based on what they see and what they learn from talking to the people involved in each event, they write a report. This they give to the newspaper editor.

The editor selects the stories that you can then read in the following day's newspaper.

Post and telegraphy

'Information technology' is a fairly new term. It's a word used to describe jointly all sorts of different methods of communication. It includes everything from the posting of letters and making a telephone call to the transmission of computer information and telex messages.

Information technology really started when the post and telegraphy systems were developed more than 100 years ago. The postal system still exists and is probably still the most far-reaching method of 'information-transfer'. It exists in every country of the world and can reach each and every individual.

Telegraphy

Telegraphy was the first electronic communications system. Radio telegraphy uses Morse code – a method of transmitting information between ships at sea. Teleprinters and the telex system are a more common form of telegraphy.

▽ A teleprinter or telex machine is often used in busy international offices. A message typed on the keyboard produces a punched paper tape. Holes in the tape represent the message in code form. The tape is fed through the machine's output unit and the code is then changed into electrical pulses. These are sent out to the receiving teleprinter, which decodes the pulses and types out the original message.

37

△ A collection of postage stamps from all over the world. Letters may bring you news of a friend, tell you that it is now time to pay the gas or electricity bill, or inform you that you have won the Pools!

◁ A letter-sorting office, where several thousand letters are processed daily by automatic sorters in the office. Envelopes are marked first with a code of tiny phosphorescent dots, each town having a specific code.

The letter-sorter robots 'read' the dots and direct the envelopes to their correct pigeon holes, read for dispatch by road, rail or air.

▷ On board a US space station an astronaut reads a teleprinter message. By means of microwave radio links, the message was transmitted to the station from NASA control on Earth within only a few minutes.

▽ The Morse code alphabet uses dots and dashes for each letter. With an electrical on-off switch-type system, messages based on this code can be sent along a wire or by radio waves. Hold the switch open for, say, a second for a 'dash' and half a second for a 'dot'.

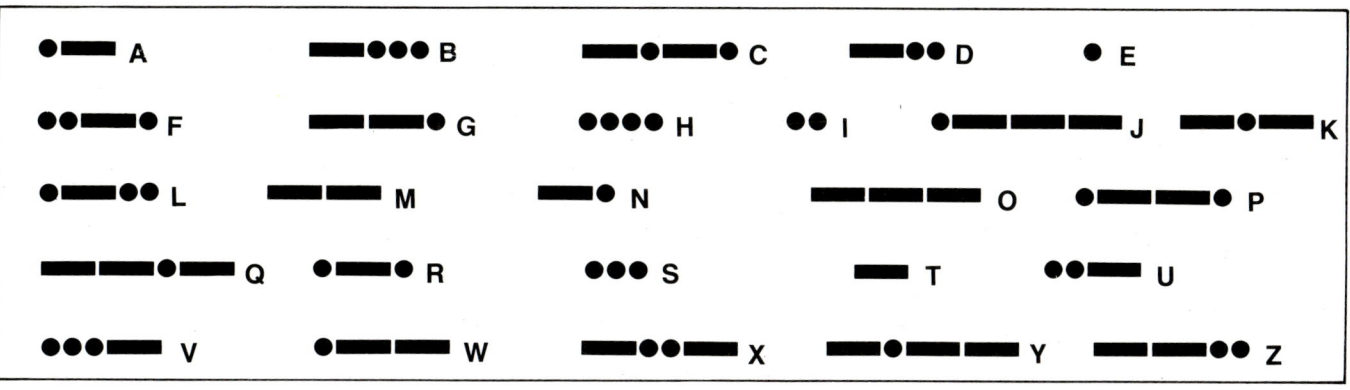

Sending Morse code messages

Use a simple electrical circuit of switch, battery and bell.

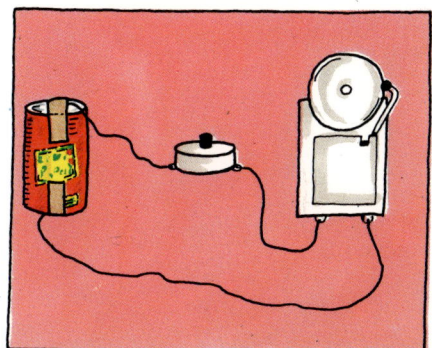

With the wire, connect up the push-button switch, bell and battery, as shown.

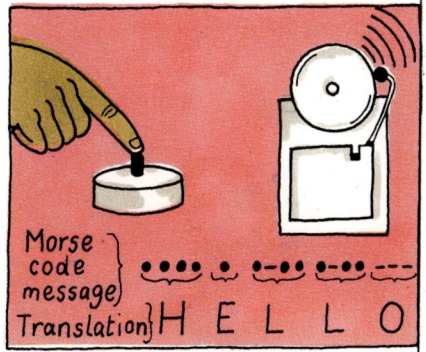

Hold the button down for the dots – short rings – and dashes – long rings.

The telephone network

Via the telephone, you can be in touch with someone on the other side of the world in less than a minute. The telephone network spanning the world consists simply of a number of single telephones, each one connected to a switching centre or telephone exchange. Local exchanges link up to regional exchanges. These in turn connect with an international telephone exchange. From here calls are directed overseas via cable or microwave radio links.

Today's telecommunication systems have been set up specifically for the telephone. A telephone is just a device for changing the sound waves of speech into electrical waves at one point and back again at another. The mouthpiece – the part of the telephone you speak into – is a simple microphone. The earpiece – the part you listen to – is a simple loudspeaker. With the development of the silicon chip, information of many different types – music, television programmes and computer data – can be transmitted through the telephone network.

Satellites and optical – fibres

Two other technological advances have dramatically changed the role of the telephone network. First, the use of satellites which can transfer digital information speedily, in great quantities and over vast distances. They also allow direct communications between homes and businesses with their own rooftop aerials. Second, optical–fibres transmit information as pulses of light. Compared to the older copper metal telephone cables, they are cheaper to make and are more efficient.

△ A computerized telephone exchange is where the electrical connections are made to make sure that a call to or from your home is routed correctly.

◁ A telephone and computer-television system. The telephone network can be used to connect you to a central computer in a supermarket. By calling up the computer, you can see on your TV a list of items in the shop. Type in your order, give your credit card and await delivery!

◁ Optical-fibre cables are made up of threads of glass each no thicker than a human hair. Information to be transmitted along such a cable – for example, a telephone conversation – is converted into pulses of laser light. This is ordinary visible light of a single, very pure colour. At the receiving end, the pulses are converted back into an electrical signal to produce the original sound message.

▷ Telephone cables can carry several thousand calls at a time. But the small, thin cable wound round the girl can carry the same number of calls as the large thick cable on the drum behind her.

The drum carries traditional copper cable, the girl new optical-fibre cable. An optical-fibre the thickness of a finger can carry a hundred television channels into your home or several thousand simultaneous telex messages and telephone calls into the head office of a large international corporation.

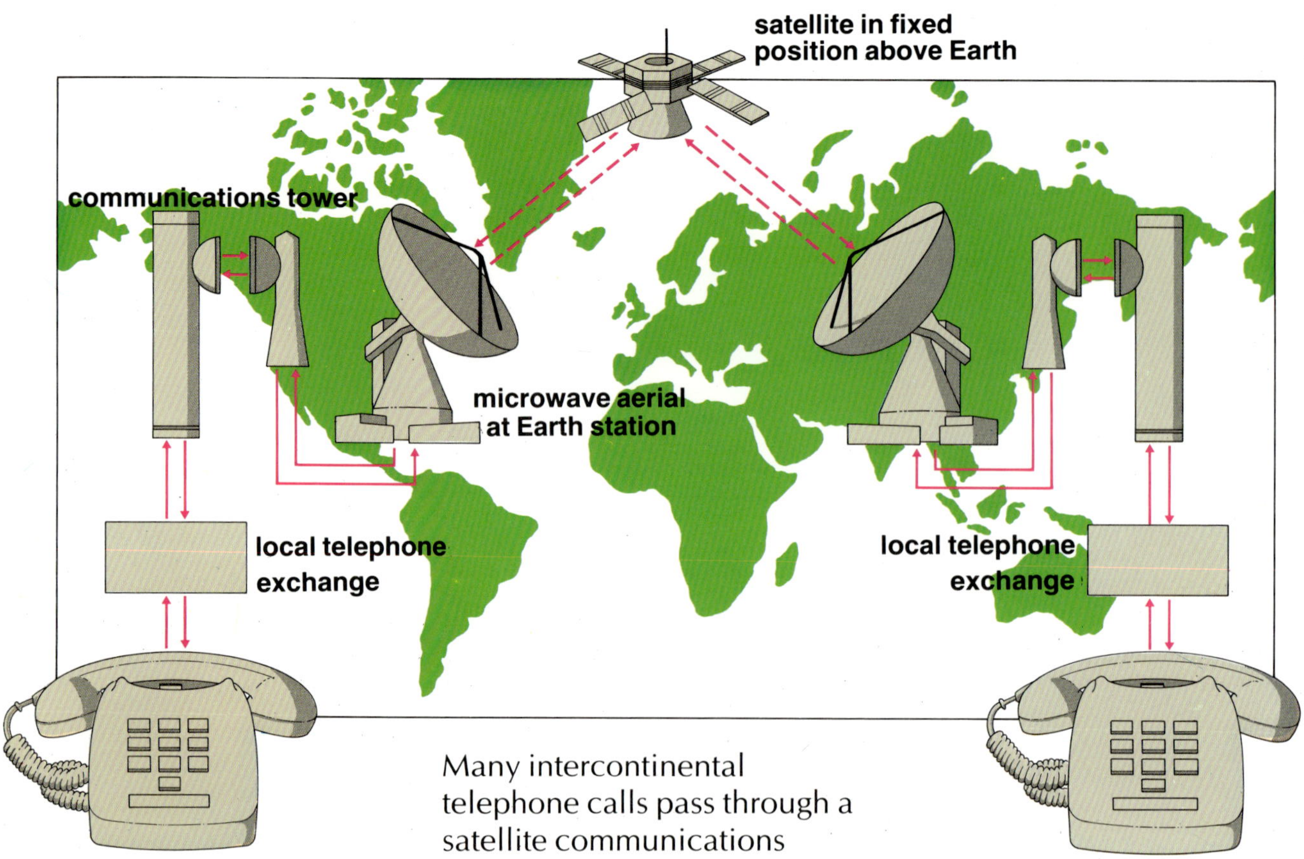

**satellite in fixed
position above Earth**

communications tower

**microwave aerial
at Earth station**

**local telephone
exchange**

**local telephone
exchange**

Many intercontinental
telephone calls pass through a
satellite communications
system. A call is first routed to
an Earth station. Next it is
beamed up to a satellite. Then
it is sent back to Earth in
another country.

telephone in home

Making a telephone call!

Feed the string through a
hole made in the base of
two yoghurt pots and secure

it using a button. Gently pull
the pots apart until the string is
tight. Each person uses a pot

as the earpiece or
mouthpiece. Whisper to
speak down the line.

Radio or 'wireless'

'Messages on the air' and 'wireless' are just the right expressions to describe radio communication. Firstly, radio signals, silently and unseen, pass through the atmosphere. Secondly, no electrical connections are involved between the source of a radio signal and the receiver.

How is this possible? Radio signals are bursts of electric current. They take the form of waves – like the waves in the sea. Radio waves have 'ups' (peaks) and 'downs' (troughs); they vary in height (amplitude) and length (wavelength).

The parts of a radio

A radio communication system has four basic parts: microphone, transmitter, receiver and loudspeaker. A 'live' microphone has a small electric current passing through it. When you speak into a microphone, the sound waves of your voice cause this background current to be altered. The louder you speak the stronger the current becomes. From the microphone, the current passes to a transmitter. When switched on, the transmitter already has an electric current passing through it. The current from the microphone is mingled with that of the transmitter and the combined current is beamed out.

On reaching a receiver – such as a transistor radio – the signal passes to a loudspeaker. Here the varying electrical current is converted back into sound waves. You hear exactly what has been spoken by someone that may be sitting on the other side of the world!

▽ The waveband display of a radio receiver. Radio waves vary in length from peak to peak, from 1,000 kilometres to only 1 millimetre. Transmitters send out radio signals of different wave-lengths so that one programme does not accidentally get mixed up with another.

The different sets of radio waves used by broadcast stations are designated SW (for short wave), MW (medium wave), LW (long wave) and VHF or FM.

Most hi-fi receivers or tuner/amplifiers can receive the complete range of signals. Some radios, such as the model from which the display shown below was taken, are not built for receiving SW signals.

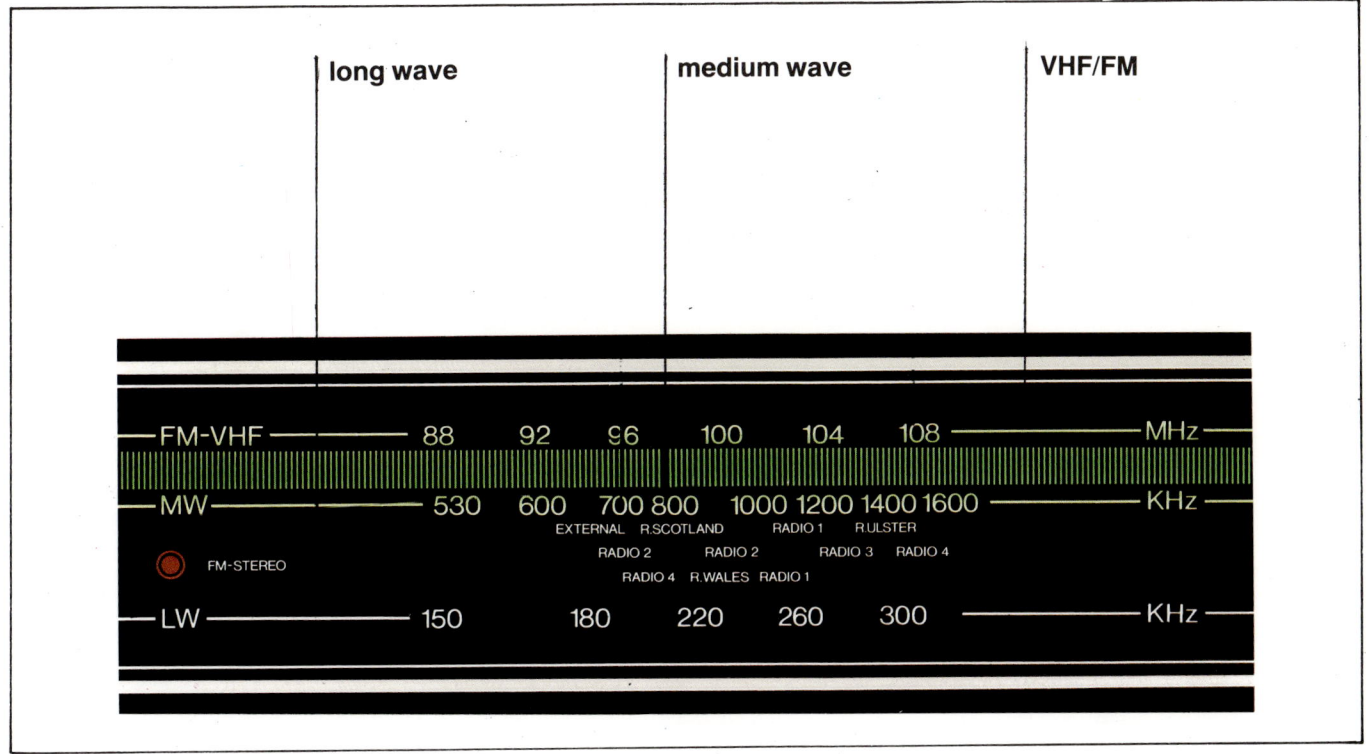

43

◁ The pop singer Toyah sings into a cordless microphone. The microphone has a small radio transmitter. Her voice is turned into radio waves that are beamed to a receiver off the stage. Via amplifiers – electronic units that magnify the strength of the radio signal – and loudspeakers, everyone in the arena can hear as she sings.

The cordless microphone is an example of the use of radio for one-way communication. Another example of this is ordinary radio broadcasting, such as Capital Radio and Radio 1. 'Walkie-talkies', radios that can be carried, are an example of two-way systems.

◁ Disc jockey Graham Dene in a Capital Radio recording studio. This is where the radio programme is created. Records played on turntables provide the music. Tapes are used for interviews with famous people and details of the day's television and sports programmes. The disc jockey provides the 'live' element – weather reports, traffic information and the 'chat'.

Microwave radio

Today, one of the most important uses of radio is that of microwave communication systems. Microwaves are radio waves with a very short wavelength – less than 30 centimetres. They can be focused into sharp beams, like light from a torch, and so do not suffer greatly from interference from other radio waves. Also, they can carry vast amounts of information. For example, most television broadcasts and almost half of Britain's trunk telephone calls are transmitted across country by microwave links between communication towers.

Microwave radio is also used for telephone systems such as 'radiopage'. A salesman may need to be contacted by his office while he is out on calls. An arranged telephone number is dialled, which automatically sets off the salesman's pocket radiopage 'bleeper'. He then 'phones his office.

▽ NASA mission control, the communications centre for all US space flights. Satellites and space vehicles such as the shuttle are equipped with microwave radio transmitters and receivers. These are used for two-way communications and for beaming down to Earth television pictures and computer information from the spacecraft.

Television

Since television began in the 1930s, it has been used mainly for watching programmes broadcast by television companies such as the BBC and ITV. It now has a second, more important job. The television is the central 'output' part for computer information systems such as teletext and viewdata.

Teletext is broadcast along with the normal television signal; viewdata is transmitted via the telephone network. Both systems have printed information and pictures displayed on the television screen. A screenful of information can be looked at for as long as one likes and then changed at the press of a button on a keypad kept next to the television set. The information – weather, road and traffic reports, sports news and current political and economic news items – is updated regularly. Teletext and viewdata together therefore may provide a better means of communication than newspapers.

Video

Programmes can be played into the television set from video cassettes and video discs. For example, instead of going to the

◁ Inside the sound control room of a TV studio. Television broadcasts consist of picture (video) and sound (audio) signals. The two signals are 'carried' by special radio waves from the broadcasting station to rooftop television aerials.

Here in the control room, the studio manager watches and listens to the programme being broadcast and makes sure that the recording level of the sound of the programme being broadcast is correctly balanced at all times.

cinema, one can hire a pre-recorded tape of the film and play it back on a video player/recorder to watch the film at home. A video camera can be used like a cine camera, so that one can take movie films of a holiday and watch them on television. Video discs can store not only films but also computer information and book reference material. The individual pages of an encyclopaedia can be viewed as still photographs on the television.

The television is as important at work and at school as it is in the home. Just as you can write letters or create pictures on the screen with your home computer, so can an office manager produce instructions on a central computer. These can be transmitted to terminals in distant departments or branches where clerks read them off their televisions or visual display units. In the same way, at airports flight arrival and departure times are displayed on giant colour television screens, the information being constantly changed and updated by computer. Using 'closed-circuit' television security staff in a bank or traffic police at a busy road junction can keep an eye on things.

△ Colour television cameras split up a picture into red, blue and green. Within home televisions, the three signals are combined to produce a picture showing the original full range of colours.

▷ A dish aerial for receiving television signals from satellites. Television signals travel in straight lines and so generally have a limited range. But by first beaming them up to a satellite, they can be transmitted thousands of kilometres away.

◁ These people are using a keypad to call up holiday information from Prestel, British Telecom's viewdata system. This computer-telephone line-television system holds the key to working, learning and shopping from home.

◁ △ A television camera perched on top of an office block films the movements of traffic at a busy crossing below. Signals from the camera are transmitted to a distant control room either via a television cable or even an ordinary telephone wire to a distant control room. Similar devices are often used by security firms in factories and large warehouses. A recent development is 'confravision'. Here business managers use the system to communicate with each other from different offices.

Tape and disc

There are two main ways of recording and playing back sound and pictures. One way uses the fact that electricity and magnetism are closely linked. If you place a compass next to an electric wire you will see that the needle lines up with the direction of the current flowing in the wire. Most sound recordings are made on plastic tape coated with a chemical.

Fluctuating sound levels, as in speech, are changed back into a fluctuating electric current. This produces a fluctuating magnetic field. On the magnetic recording tape, a pattern is produced that reflects the original sound pattern. When the tape is run through a playback machine, the opposite happens and the spoken message is reproduced.

Ultramodern disc recording and playback systems use the connection between light and electricity. A camera light meter, for example, contains a number of 'photoelectric' cells. When light rays strike the cells a current is produced and the meter moves. The recording is made on a disc (usually via a master tape) and appears as tiny pits. The length and distance between the pits carries the sound and visual information.

△ The film library of the BBC. All television programmes are recorded on videotape. This is both for retelevising at a later date and for making copies for sale to other broadcasting companies or as videotapes for home use. The sound and visual signals are stored on the tape in magnetic form.

Because the tapes are badly affected by heat, dust, strong light and dampness, they are stored here in metal cans in a darkened, airy room.

◁ Inside the control room of a record recording studio. To make a record, the original sound – a pop song, a play or an opera, for example – is first recorded on magnetic tape. From this a master disc is made. The records you buy are pressed from this master disc.

Records and videodiscs

The first step in making a record is the production of the original soundtrack. Studio tape recorders use wide tapes that may store as many as 24 individual tracks. During the recording of a pop song, for instance, a separate track may be used for each microphone signal. The lead singer's voice, the lead and rhythm guitarists' chords and the drummers' beats will then, as separate tape tracks, be mixed together as the record producer wishes. In this way, too old 'mono' recordings can be remade in 'stereo' by simply mixing the original soundtrack with new additional tracks.

Videodiscs record both sound and pictures. In one such system, Philips Laservision, the recording consists of a single spiral track of discreet pits in the disc's surface. To play it back, the disc is scanned by a laser beam.

Laservision and Selectavision

In another system, RCA Selectavision, the disc has a fine groove of pits. Here the pits carry the original recording in the form of a varying capacity to store electric current. A needle or stylus tracks across the disc, sensing the changes in the electrical property of the disc's surface which is brought about by the differing pits.

A great advantage of the Laservision system is that each turn of the disc gives a fixed number of television picture frames. Each of the frames can be called up individually on screen within seconds, making it possible to see still pictures. This is the basis of photo and text libraries.

Another good thing about the Laservision system is that the pickup never makes physical contact with the disc. The discs can never wear out.

◁ A modern home stereo hi-fi system. This includes a cassette tape recorder and player, a record or disc turntable, a radio or tuner, an amplifier and two loudspeakers. Video players are now replacing the record player unit.

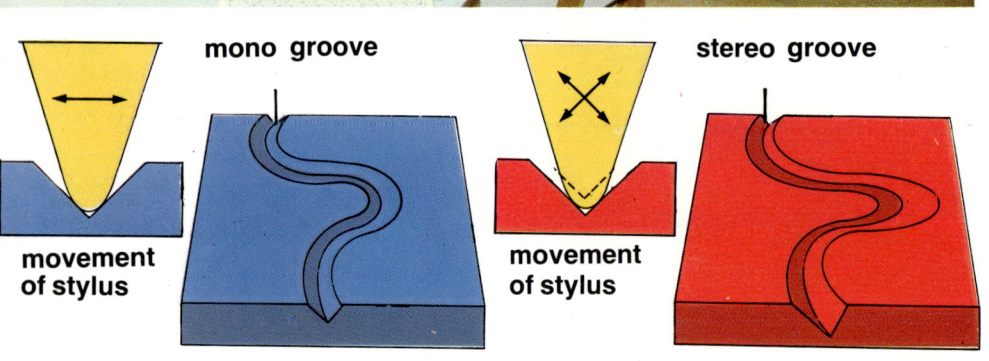

◁ Mono and stereo record tracks. The wave-like pattern of a record groove carries the original sound recording in coded form. With a mono record, the groove is of constant width and depth. As the record turns, the stylus moves from side to side. With a stereo record, the stylus moves up and down and from side to side. This produces two sound signals.

▷ A home video recorder and player. Ordinary tape recorders can store on tape only sound signals. A video recorder tape system can store both sound and picture signals. You can record a television programme on, say, BBC1 while watching Channel 4, and play it back just when you like.

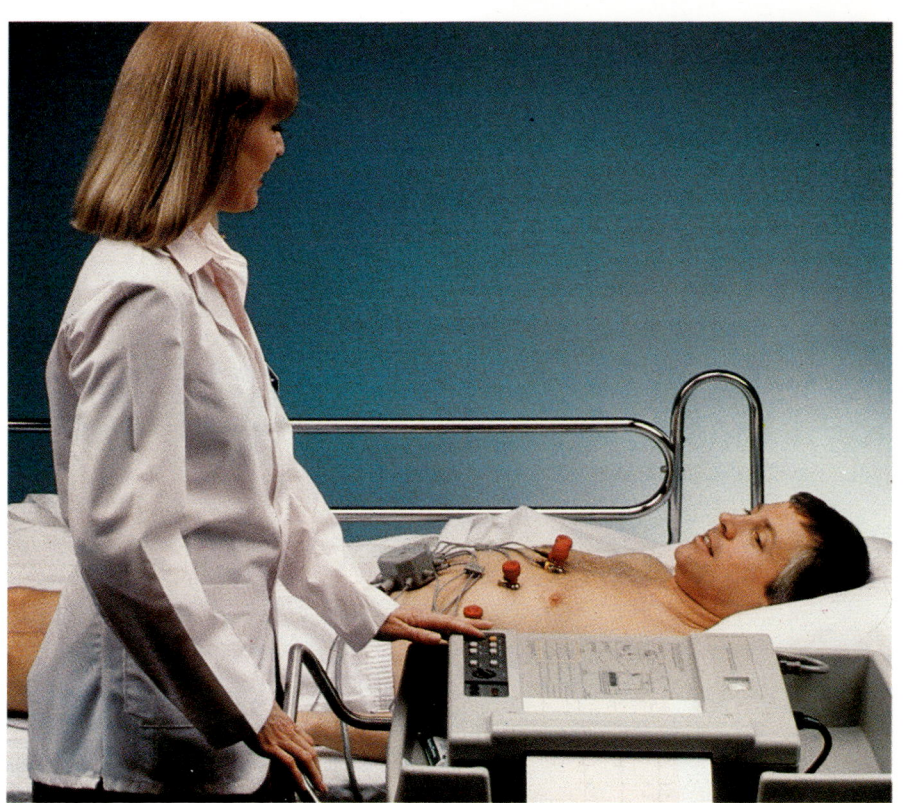

◁ A patient connected to an electrocardiograph machine. This records the electrical activity of the heart. But instead of using a magnetic tape or videodisc, it uses a plain paper tape. Metal contacts are taped on to the person's chest. They are connected by wires to the electrocardiograph. Signals from the heart control the movement of an electrically driven pen under which the paper tape is fed. The pen moves across the tape to produce a wave-like pattern.

The 'tape recording' is known as an electrocardiogram or ECG. The recording can be viewed on a television screen.

Cameras and film

Photographic film uses a special chemical that changes colour or form in some way when exposed to light. A camera is needed to focus the light rays from part of a scene onto the film.

How a camera works

The camera is basically a lens on one side of a box that projects an image onto the box's opposite side, where the film is placed. The camera has a shutter – a blind that is temporarily removed from in front of the film when a picture is taken. It also has a diaphragm – an arrangement of metal blades that change the working size of the lens. These control the amount of light that reaches the film. 'Overexposure' results in a featureless, white-washed image. 'Underexposure' produces a grey, overcast picture.

Today there is film that is also sensitive to invisible X-rays, infra-red or heat rays and other types of radiation.

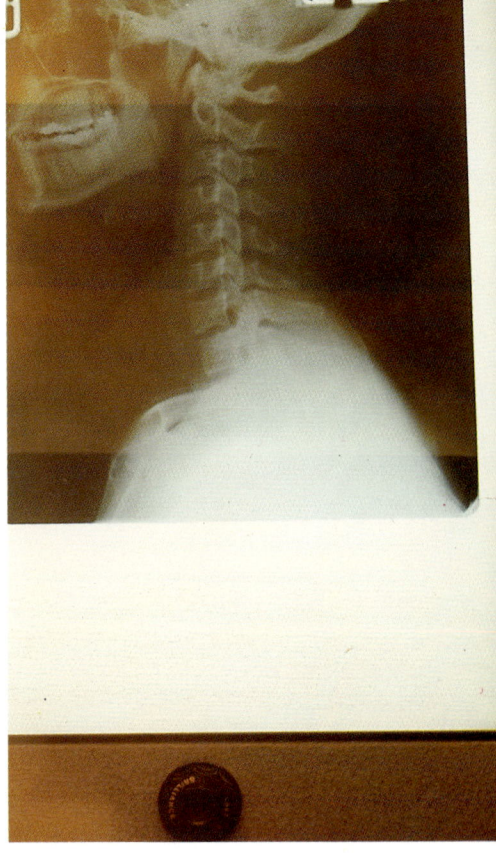

△ An X-ray picture of a live person's neck and head. X-rays can pass through the skin and muscles but less easily through bones.

◁ This three-dimensional image of a cup was taken using a photographic technique known as holography. A beam of laser light – visible light of a single, very pure colour – is split.

The two halves of the beam are each focused through lenses and reflected by mirrors. They are then made to combine again on a special photographic plate. If laser light is shone through the plate, the object is re-created so that it looks real.

▷ Looking at the screen of a microfiche reader. Microfiche is a sheet of film, usually about the size of a postcard, that is used in a special camera to copy a large number of documents and similar materials so that the information can be stored.

The 'originals' – pages from a book, photographs, company records, for example – are laid out flat and the photograph taken. To see any detail the developed film must be looked at under a 'viewer'.

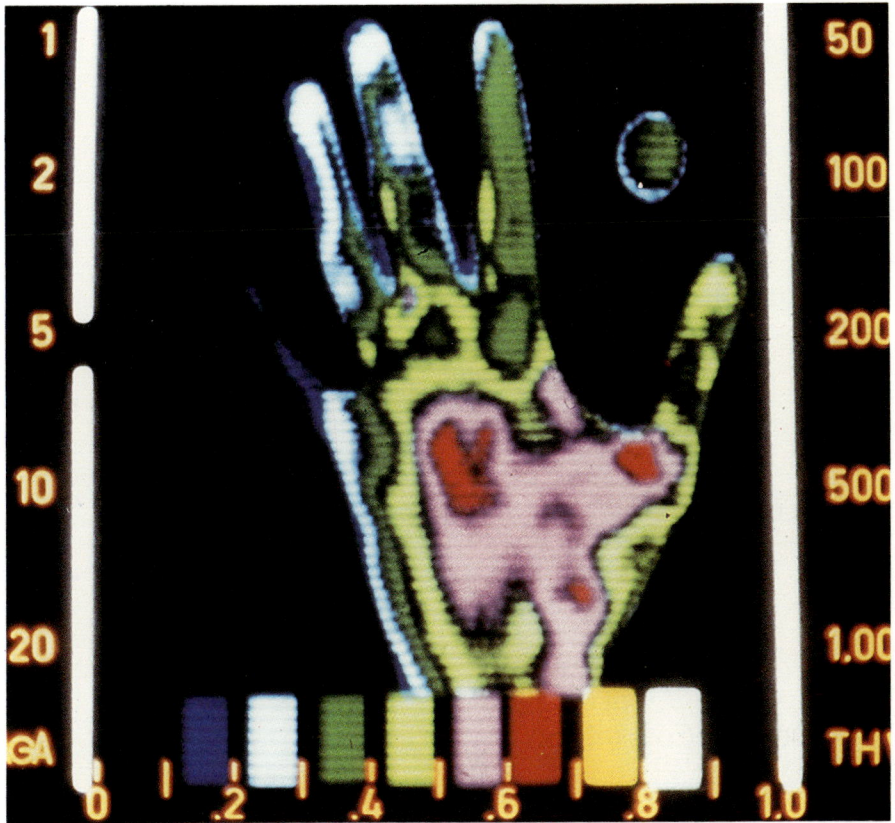

◁ A photo of a hand taken with infra-red or heat-sensitive film. Instead of recording the lightest and darkest parts of an object, infra-red film records the hottest and coldest. In this artificially coloured photo, blue represents very cold and yellow and white very warm.

Infra-red photography has many uses. In medicine it can detect diseased or damaged areas of the body. Compared to healthy tissue, these areas are warmer and so show as dark zones on the film.

In architecture, infra-red is used to find out where heat is lost from buildings. An infra-red photo of a house will show blue areas around the windows, doors and the roof.

◁ Underwater photography poses several problems. First, the deeper one dives, the greater the pressure of the water on the camera (and the diver). An underwater camera must be sturdily built and, of course, be fully waterproof.

Second, as light rays pass from the water into the lens of the camera they become bent. This makes objects underwater appear closer and larger than they really are. One must allow for this when estimating how much of a scene one will capture on the film. Third, within a metre or two of the surface of the water, it is very dark and so a flash gun is needed to provide sufficient light.

Make a pinhole camera!

Cut off the lid of a box. Cover the open end with greaseproof paper.

At the other end, cut out a small square. Cover this with foil. Make a pinhole in the foil.

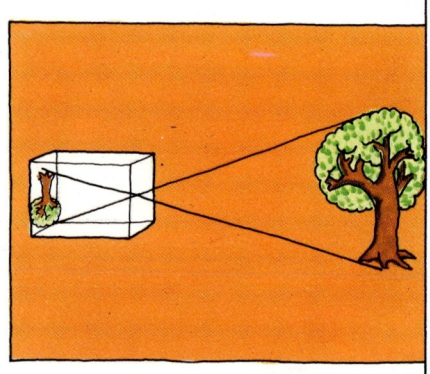

Focus the 'camera' on an object. The image will appear on the 'screen'.

Sight and sound

Systems that provide the brain with sound (audio) and picture (visual) messages together are very powerful means of communication. The dramatic way in which television took over from radio and then movie films killed off silent movies clearly shows this.

At school, the simplest of these audio-visual techniques is the combination of teacher and blackboard. Another is a projector slide show with commentary or background music played through an ordinary cassette player. This is the sort of set-up that you yourself might use at home to present to your family and friends the story of your holiday or school trip. You might also have at school a microcomputer system. The television is the output on which edu-

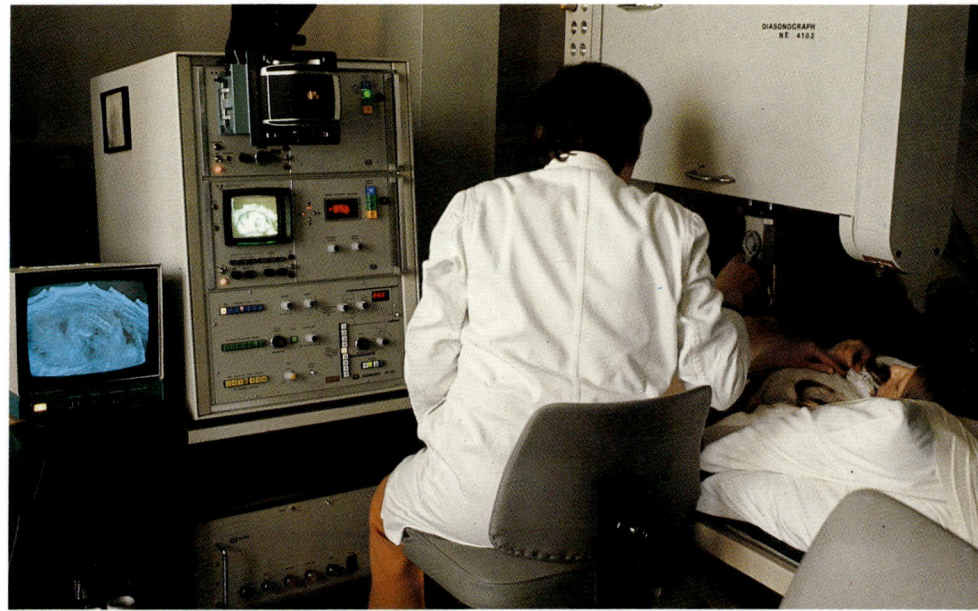

▷ A doctor checks the size and position of a foetus inside a mother's womb using an ultrasound body scanner. High-pitched sound waves are projected onto the mother's abdomen. They pass through her body and are reflected by bones, muscles, body fluids and so on. The reflections are converted electronically into a picture showing the foetus inside the womb.

▷ A multi-projector giant-screen slide show-and-tape recorder sound system. Such audio-visual presentations are widely used in advertizing and sales. The projectors are linked to a computer that programs them to work together to produce a single huge picture. Or the computer may make them work independently to form a pattern of separate images.

The computer also synchronizes sound and pictures – that is it makes sure that the slides in the projectors are changed in time with the soundtrack.

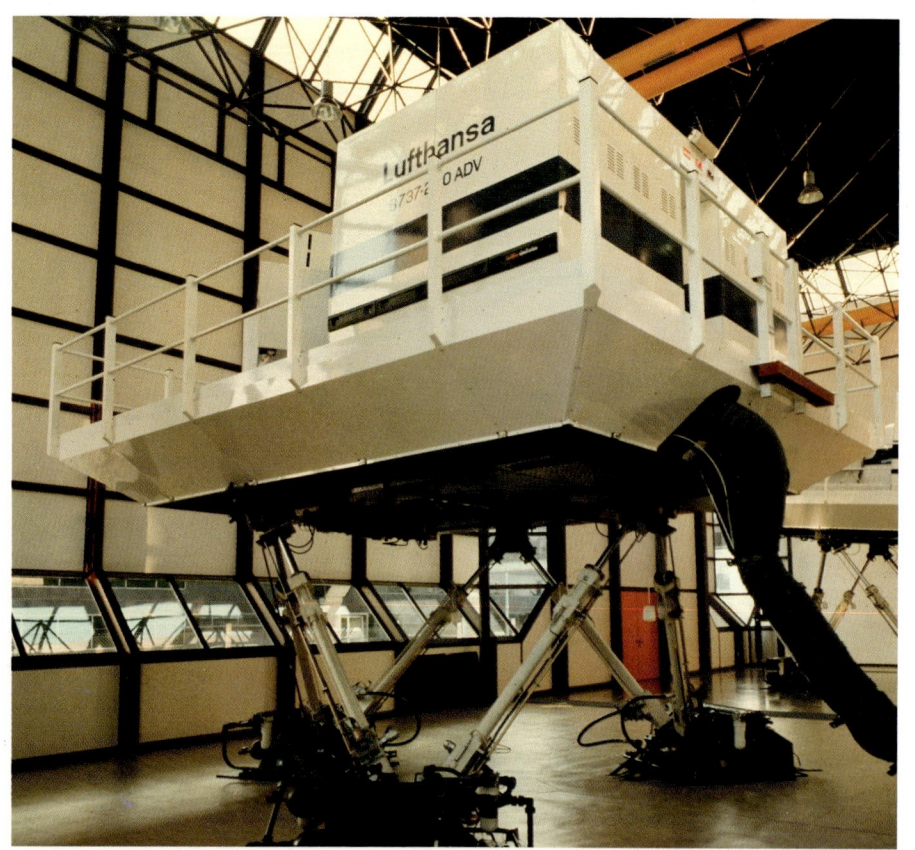

◁ A Boeing 737 jet airliner flight simulator. In the simulator, airline pilots can learn to fly without ever leaving the ground. Inside the cabin is a model flight deck. All the instrument panels, switches and pieces of flight control equipment found on the real 737 are here and they all work.

A light-projector system produces a realistic view through the cockpit window. A loudspeaker system provides the sound of the aircraft's engines. The cabin itself is mounted on hydraulic arms so that it can tilt and rotate like the actual aircraft.

◁ Looking over the pilot and co-pilot's shoulders in the flight deck of the simulator.

The simulator's joystick and wing and tailplane flap controls are linked to a computer. As they are operated by the pilots they alter the position in space of the simulator cabin, copying the real-life situation. The computer also alters the aircraft's engine noise and instruments.

Here the 'aircraft' is making its approach to the airport runway.

cational games, using both graphics and sounds, are played.

Audio-visual aids are used not only in schools but also in colleges, universities and sports centres. Perhaps the most widely used aids are the closed circuit television and video recorder systems. With a video camera, a football instructor, for example, can film his players while they train. The film can then be played back at anytime, stopping where necessary to allow the players to study their own progress and development.

The hiring or buying of video cassettes with instructional films and soundtrack makes learning almost anything at home possible. The educational programmes used by the Open University on BBC television are another example of audio-visuals for the home.

Planetariums

Planetariums also use audio-visual systems. At the centre of the dome there is a projector complex that creates the starry sky on the ceiling. A tape recorder provides the commentary or music. Visually, planetariums copy or 'simulate' the real-life situation. It is with simulations, in fact, that audio-visual techniques are especially effective. You can learn how to drive, fly the space shuttle, play golf or spend a day in Paris, all inside a 'sight and sound' simulation cabin.

▷ A scene from *Laserium*, a laser light-and-sound show. An ordinary light bulb produces light made up of all the colours of the rainbow. Also, the light spreads out in all directions from the bulb.

A laser is a light source that produces a very powerful, pencil-like beam of light of only one colour. Visually, laser light can produce some stunning images, as here.

The beams from several laser 'guns' can be merged together and focused on any one point to produce pictures that seem to hang in mid-air. Music, played in time with ever-changing laser images, creates a truly 'audio-visual experience'. Many pop groups use laser light shows to accompany their live concerts.

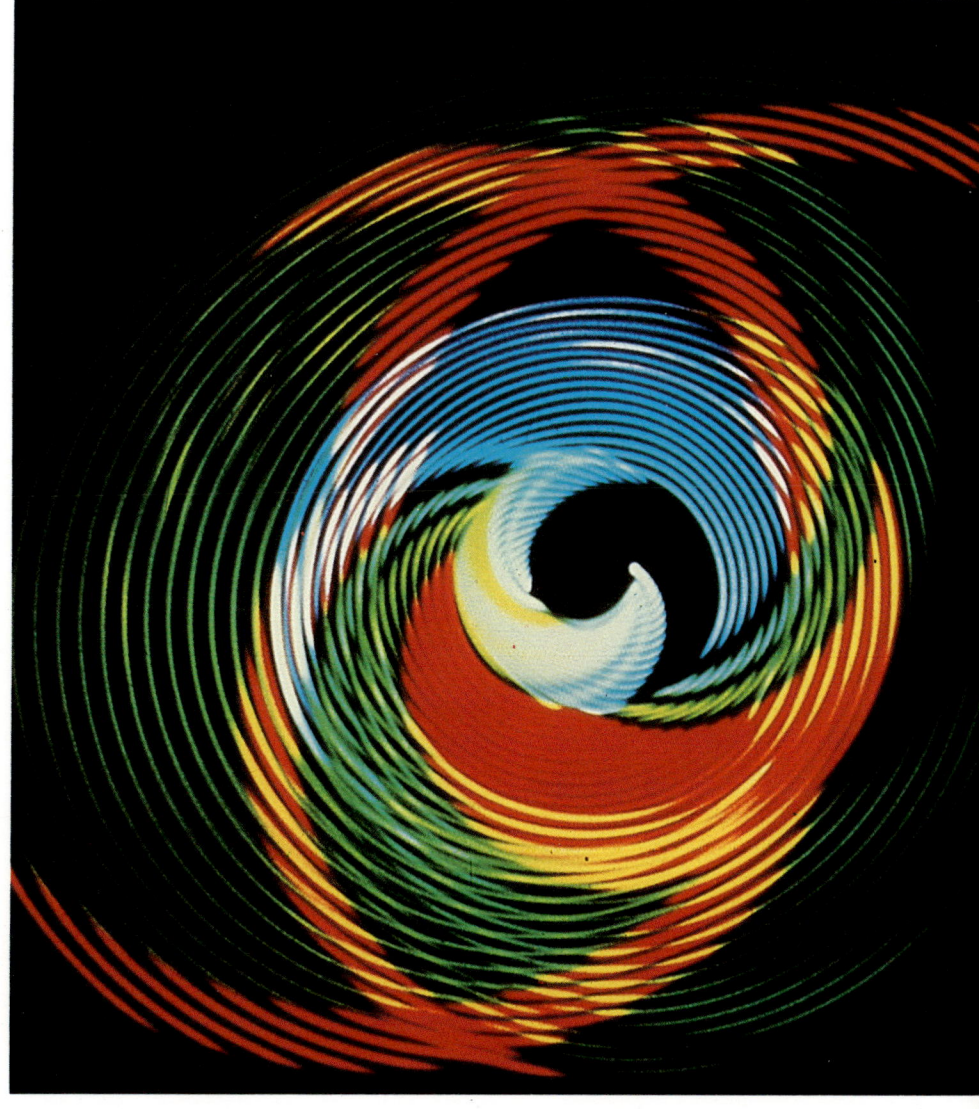

Robot systems

Robots are machines controlled by computers. They are used to perform jobs too difficult, too dangerous or simply too tedious for we humans to do. Robots can work non-stop 24 hours a day. They never tire and they don't get bored. They can work more efficiently, accurately and to a higher standard than people. They can work in hot, dry, dusty, dark and underwater conditions.

Programming robots

Before a robot can do anything its computer must be suitably programmed. It needs a human instructor. However, a robot can be taught a considerable amount. Instructions can be built into the design of its computer memory so that much of its work is automatic. For example, a robot can be programmed to pick up an object from a production line, put it in a box then return to the line. It can be instructed to do this 100 times, until the box is full. The only truly 'intelligent' operation the robot then does is to switch itself off on reaching the 101st object.

▽ Lowering a deep-water telephone cable repair robot, *Scarab 1*, into the sea from a cable-laying ship. The robot is fitted with two mechanical arms, underwater TV cameras, lights and several computer control systems. It is operated from the deck of the ship. It skims along the sea-bed, electronically following the track of a buried cable. When it finds a damaged or cut piece of cable, it can attach lines for lifting the cable up to the ship.

As electronics and computing improve, so too will the capabilities of robots. Already, in some factories communications systems have been developed between robots and other machines so that a process is fully automated. Industrial robots can now be programmed simply by being given a 'lesson'.

For example, a robot that sprays paint on car bodies has a mechanical arm unit with a spray gun attached to its wrist. The arm can be moved freely and continuously over the surface to be painted. The human operator starts up the robot's control system memory and then moves the arm just as if he were painting the car. The memory unit records the moves in the correct order. Taught in just one lesson, the robot faithfully reproduces the arm movements whenever commanded to do so.

The future

In science fiction we are told that in the 21st century we will all be sitting at home in front of our computers and televisions operating human-like robots. These will do all the housework, service and repair the car and all electrical appliances and generally look after us. Using telephone and television links, business managers will control robots in distant production plants and electronic offices.

This may not be so far from the truth. The technology which could allow us to live like this is only a few years away. Whether it happens or not will depend mainly on how much we value our current life-style.

△ A robot soil-sampler aboard the US spacecraft Viking tries to scoop up a specimen of soil from Mars. Viking was unmanned.

All the mechanical operations were carried out by robot units controlled from NASA on Earth.

◁ Dr Who's faithful robot K9. Fitted with a computer, it can talk and do sums. Other famous robots of film and TV include the Daleks and the heroes of *Star Wars*, R2D2 and C3P0. Robots that look like human beings, such as C3P0, are known as androids.

▷ Robots at work on the *Sierra* production line at Ford's car assembly plant. Controlled by computers, the machines weld together parts of the car body and spray them with paint. Other robots tighten nuts and drill holes in the engine block.

Robots can be fitted with 'sensors' to perform more complex jobs. For example, a light sensitive 'eye' unit can be programmed to direct the robot's cutting arm along a line. In this way pieces of metal of different shapes can be cut from a single sheet on which the outlines have been marked.

◁ Examining the nuclear fuel elements at an atomic power station. The fuel elements are very radioactive. Radioactivity is extremely dangerous, so the rods are stored in a room with a thick protective concrete wall. To inspect the rods, the examiner operates the mechanical arms and hands using a computer-controlled guidance system. In this way the rods are never handled directly.

Robots are used in other dangerous situations, such as coalmines, the cutting of underground tunnels and deep ocean geological and biological studies.

Space communication and control

Normal television transmissions have a range of only a few hundred kilometres. Many radio broadcasts can travel even less distance than this. Telephone links between major cities mean the laying underground of tens of thousands of kilometres of cable.

Nowadays, it is much more costly to build a system of transmitters the length and breadth of a country and to establish complex cable networks than it is to launch a satellite or two. It is especially important for small and developing nations to remember this, as many of them still do not have extensive nationwide communications systems.

Microwave radio links used to carry telephone circuits and to distribute television programmes around the country mean that giant aerials have to be built every 50 kilometres. London's 200-metre high Telecom Tower is the centre of a network of 200 of these aerials. A small number of satellites and ground based communications stations can do exactly the same job and provide a means of contact with the rest of the world.

Satellites and their uses

Communications satellites and space stations are certainly the answer to the ever-increasing demand for telephone, television and computer links between nations. They are also the best means of keeping an eye on the activities and movements of people, for monitoring the weather and for surveying the land. Some of these activities can be very helpful to us. By observing the build-up of clouds we can predict severe storms. Using satellites with infra-red cameras, we can photograph vast areas of land and sea to look for signs of pollution or disease within vegetation. Oil companies searching for ideal places to drill can be sure of finding the right bit of rock.

▷ US astronaut Musgrave makes a routine check on retro rockets outside his spacecraft. The rockets control movement of the craft in space. Within such craft, astronauts live in a pressurized, air-filled compartment. By means of radio links they can communicate with mission control on Earth.

Before an astronaut can step outside into space, he must put on a spacesuit. This provides cooling and pressurization and protects against radiation and being hit by tiny meteorites. A safety rope makes sure the astronaut cannot be separated from the craft. Learning to work outside the craft is essential for the astronaut who will service and repair it.

Depending on their use, satellites are placed in one of two types of orbit round the Earth. A communications satellite used to beam television pictures and telephone messages between, say, London and New York, is sent up to a height of 36,000 kilometres above the Earth.

Here it orbits the Earth every 24 hours. This is the time it takes for the Earth to rotate once on its axis. The result is that the satellite appears to be in a fixed position in the sky. Antennae at ground stations can point continuously at the same spot above the Earth.

Weather satellites

Some weather satellites, on the other hand, are put into a much lower orbit, only about 800 kilometres above the Earth's surface. They do not remain over the same point on Earth but circle it every two hours or so. The satellite passes over a different point on Earth each time because it is launched in such a way that each orbit is further east or west than the previous one. A typical weather satellite has cameras which can cover the whole globe once every 12 or 24 hours.

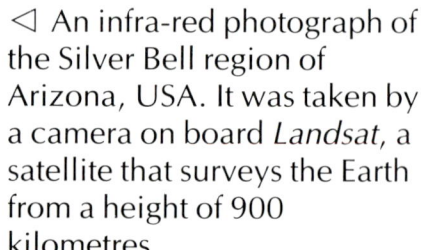

◁ An infra-red photograph of the Silver Bell region of Arizona, USA. It was taken by a camera on board *Landsat*, a satellite that surveys the Earth from a height of 900 kilometres.

Landsat circles the Earth more than ten times a day, passing over a different strip of land each orbit. Its cameras send back photographs of slightly overlapping areas of land to tracking stations. The photographs are in coded form. In this way a total picture of the globe is built up.

Infra-red film is sensitive to heat rays. Different types of rock and soil, polluted and clear water and healthy and diseased vegetation radiate different amounts of heat.

▷ This is the Earth station communication complex at Ras Abu Jarjur, Bahrain.

The two giant dishes (antennae or aerials) link up via microwave radio with satellites orbiting the Earth. They are part of an international telephone, telegraph, telex, television and computer network that spans the globe. A telecommunication tower such as this is the centre of a nationwide system.

▷ The *Transit* satellite navigation system as used by a ship at sea.

As a *Transit* satellite passes over the ship, a computer linked to a special receiving aerial records, for example, three positions of the satellite. It also records the time interval between receiving these three signals. The computer can then accurately work out the ship's position. On land, a tracking station, a transmitter and a computer centre work together to update the information the satellite sends to ships.

The future in space

Space holds the key for all future communication and control. But launching satellite and space probes costs several hundreds of millions of pounds. It is hoped that the space shuttle, a re-usable manned spacecraft, will overcome some of the many problems.

Until the shuttle, all space rockets burned away during or soon after a launch. The shuttle is designed to be used 100 times. In its cargo bay, the shuttle can carry several satellites at once. Fitted with a remote control arm, it can retrieve satellites for inspection and repair or bring worn out spacecraft back to Earth. Finally, the shuttle is bringing together nations interested in launching spacecraft.

◁ The first space shuttle flight, April 12, 1981. On board were astronauts Young and Crippen. The spacecraft stands 56 metres high and weighs more than 2,000 tonnes. The orbiter itself is the size of a large airplane. Half its length is taken up by a cargo bay capable of carrying 29 tonnes of equipment into space.

Two minutes after launch of the shuttle, the two solid fuel rocket boosters burn out and are separated from the craft. They parachute into the sea and are recovered for re-use.

Next to burn out is the giant external fuel tank. This is the only part of the shuttle that cannot be re-used. As it drops from the craft it burns up in the atmosphere. The orbiter is now on its own. It enters a circular orbit some 180 kilometres above the Earth. To return to Earth, thrusters on the shuttle are fired to slow it down and take it out of orbit and gradually down through the atmosphere.

Index